42 

Calming the Storm

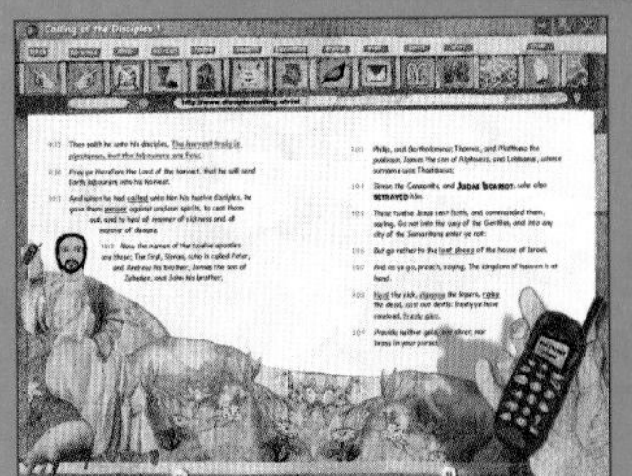 52

Calling of the Disciples

80 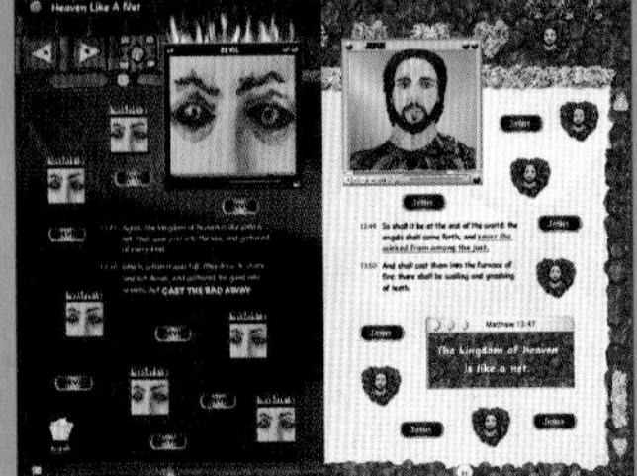

Heaven Like A Net

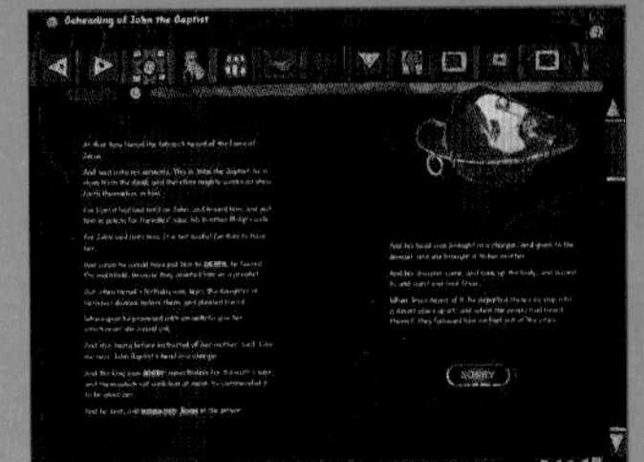 84

Beheading of the Baptist

88 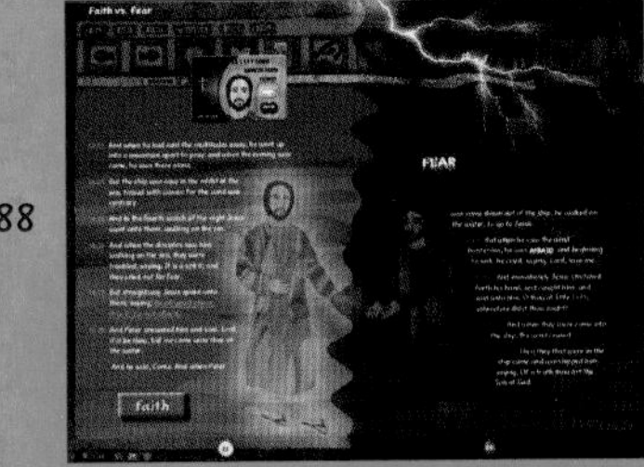

Faith vs. Fear

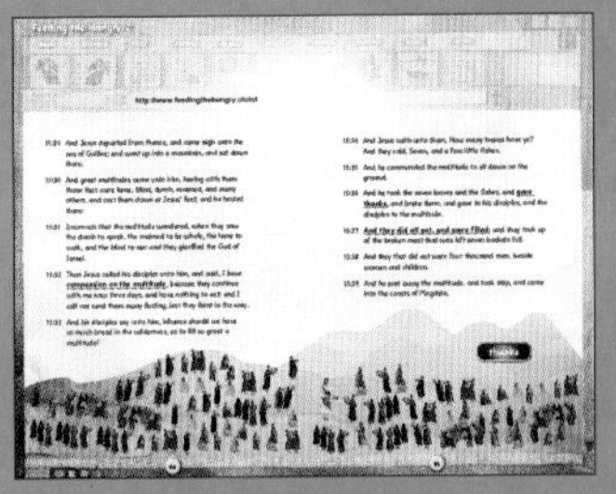 94

Feeding the Hungry

96 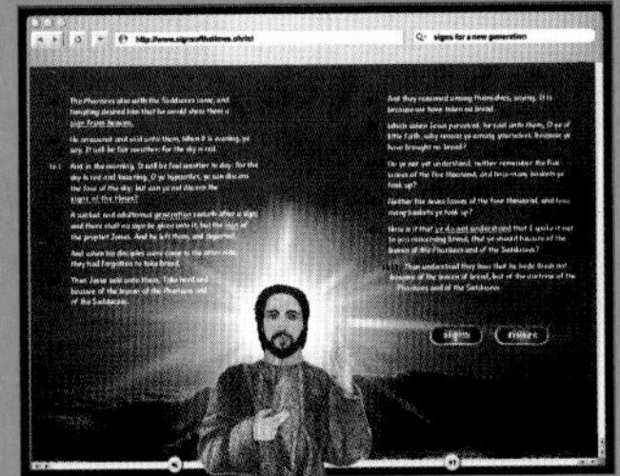

Signs of the Times

 98

Keys to the Kingdom

.Christ™

The Gospel of Matthew
Beautifully Designed for the Internet Age

King James Version

With the Book of Ruth and A Testimony for Christ

Art Direction and Design:
Ruth Rimm

Illustrations:
Alejandra Vernon

First volume in the Designer Bible™ series
Published by The Global Renaissance Society, LLC
New York

www.dotchrist.net

For more information, please visit the publisher's website at **www.dotchrist.net.** Permission requests should be sent to permissions@dotchrist.net.

Ruth Rimm can be reached at ruth@dotchrist.net
Alejandra Vernon can be reached at alejandra@dotchrist.net

 Footnotes for the citations and a complete bibliography are provided in *Goodbye Gutenberg*.

First edition
ISBN: 0-9745750-4-6

This edition is distributed by
Executive Books
206 West Allen Street
Mechanicsburg, PA 17055
717-766-9499 800-233-2665
Fax: 717-766-6565
www.executivebooks.com

Manufactured in China

To Gloria

and

Charlie "Tremendous" Jones

"Let your light so shine before men,
that they may see your good works,
and glorify your Father in Heaven."

Matthew 5:16

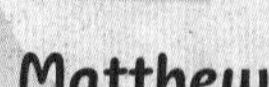

Matthew

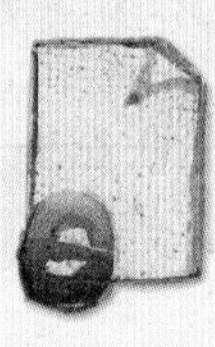

Ruth

Testimony for Christ

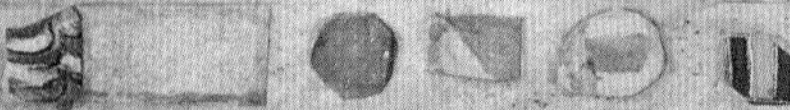

Matthew

turn to enter

Genealogy of Christ

1:1

The book of the generation of Jesus Christ, the son of David, the son of Abraham.

1:2 Abraham begat Isaac; and Isaac begat Jacob; and Jacob begat Judas and his brethren;

1:3 And Judas begat Phares and Zara of Thamar; and Phares begat Esrom; and Esrom begat Aram;

1:4 And Aram begat Aminadab; and Aminadab begat Naasson; and Naasson begat Salmon;

1:5 And Salmon begat Boaz of Rachab; and Boaz begat Obed of Ruth and Obed begat Jesse;

1:6 And Jesse begat David the king; and David the king begat Solomon of her that had been the wife of Urias;

1:7 And Solomon begat Roboam; and Roboam begat Abia; and Abia begat Asa;

1:8 And Asa begat Josaphat; and Josaphat begat Joram; and Joram begat Ozias;

1:9 And Ozias begat Joatham; and Joatham begat Achaz; and Achaz begat Ezekias;

1:10 And Ezekias begat Manasses; and Manasses begat Amon; and Amon begat Josias;

1:11 And Josias begat Jechonias and his brethren, about the time they were carried away to Babylon:

1:12 And after they were brought to Babylon, Jechonias begat Salathiel; and Salathiel begat Zorobabel;

1:13 And Zorobabel begat Abiud; and Abiud begat Eliakim; and Eliakim begat Azor;

1:14 And Azor begat Sadoc; and Sadoc begat Achim; and Achim begat Eliud;

1:15 And Eliud begat Eleazar; and Eleazar begat Matthan; and Matthan begat Jacob;

1:16 And Jacob begat Joseph the husband of Mary, of whom was born Jesus, who is called **Christ.**

1:17 So all the generations from Abraham to David are fourteen generations; and from David until the carrying away into Babylon are fourteen generations; and from the carrying away into Babylon unto Christ are fourteen generations.

back forward stop grace home search

http://www.madonna.christ

1:18 Now the birth of Jesus Christ was on this wise: When as his mother Mary was espoused to Joseph, before they came together, she was found with child of the **Holy Ghost**.

1:19 Then Joseph her husband, being a just man, and not willing to make her a publick example, was minded to put her away privily.

1:20 But while he thought on these things, behold, the angel of the Lord appeared unto him in a dream, saying, Joseph, thou son of David, fear not to take unto thee Mary thy wife: for that which is conceived in her is of the **Holy Ghost**.

1:21 And she shall bring forth a son, and thou shalt call his name **Jesus**: for he shall save his people from their sins.

1:22 Now all this was done, that it might be fulfilled which was spoken of the Lord by the prophet, saying,

1:23 Behold, a virgin shall be with child, and shall bring forth a son, and they shall call his name Emmanuel, which being interpreted is, **God with us**.

1:24 Then Joseph being raised from sleep did as the angel of the Lord had bidden him, and took unto him his wife:

1:25 And knew her not till she had brought forth her firstborn son: and he called his name **Jesus**.

2:1 Now when Jesus was born in Bethlehem of Judaea in the days of Herod the king, behold, there came wise men from the east to Jerusalem,

2:2 Saying, Where is he that is born King of the Jews? for we have seen his star in the east, and are come to **worship** him.

2:3 When Herod the king had heard these things, he was troubled, and all Jerusalem with him.

2:4 And when he had gathered all the chief priests and scribes of the people together, he demanded of them where Christ should be born.

2:5 And they said unto him, In Bethlehem of Judaea: for thus it is written by the prophet,

2:6 And thou Bethlehem, in the land of Juda, art not the least among the princes of Juda: for out of thee shall come a Governor, that shall rule my people Israel.

2:7 Then Herod, when he had privily called the wise men,
enquired of them diligently what time the star appeared.

2:8 And he sent them to Bethlehem, and said, Go and search
diligently for the young child; and when ye have found him,
bring me word again, that I may come and worship him
also.

2:9 When they had heard the king, they departed; and, lo, the
star, which they saw in the east, went before them, till it
came and stood over where the young child was.

2:10 When they saw the star, they rejoiced with exceeding great
joy.

2:11 And when they were come into the house, they saw the
young child with Mary his mother, and fell down, and
worshipped him: and when they had opened their
treasures, they presented unto him gifts;

2:12 And being warned of God in a dream that they should
not return to Herod, they departed into their own
country another way.

2:13 And when they were departed, behold, the angel of
the Lord appeareth to Joseph in a dream, saying,
Arise, and take the young child and his mother, and
flee into Egypt, and be thou there until I bring thee
word: for Herod will seek the young child to
destroy him.

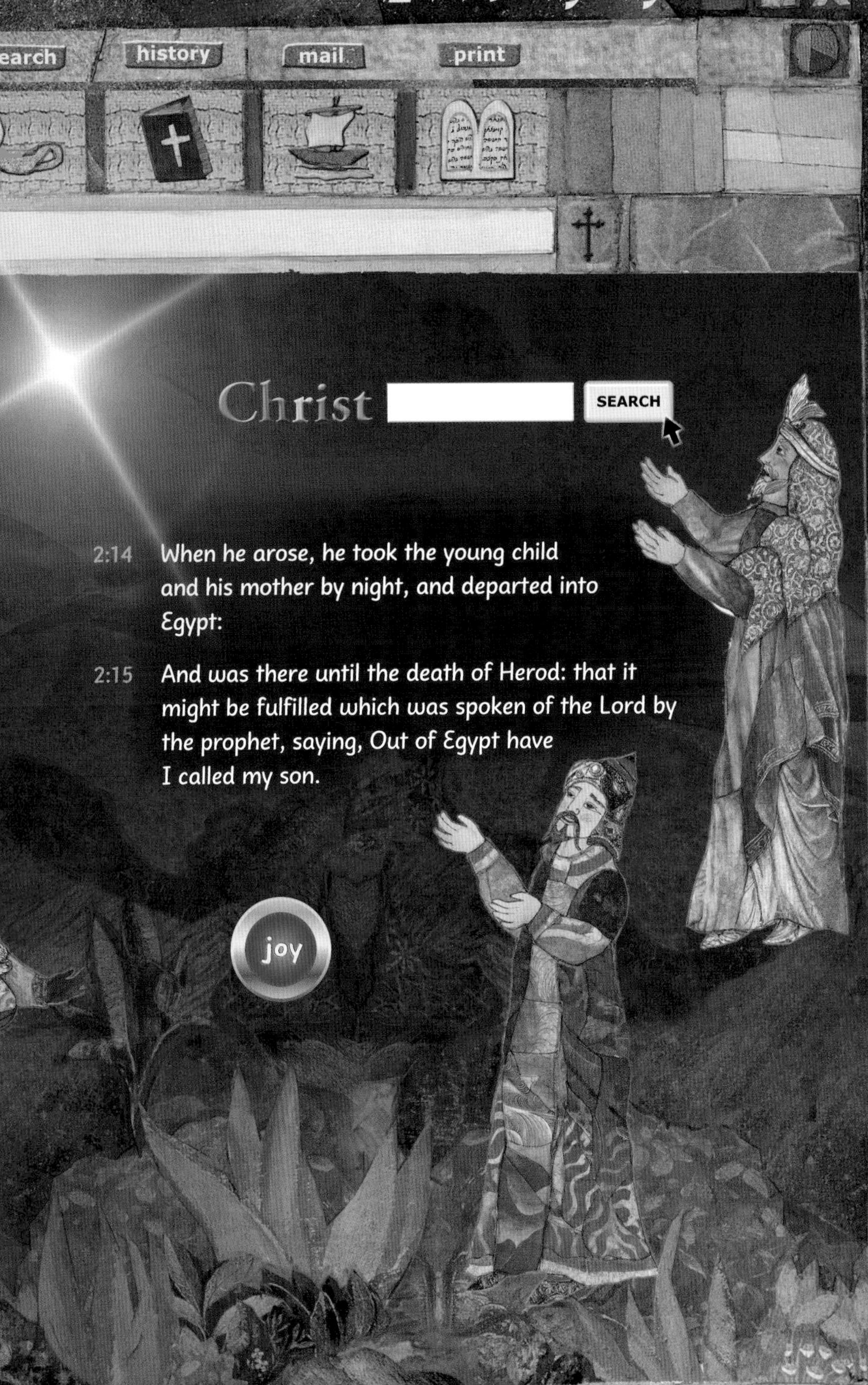

עורי עורי שיר דברי
earch
history
mail
print
Christ
SEARCH
2:14 When he arose, he took the young child
and his mother by night, and departed into
Egypt:
2:15 And was there until the death of Herod: that it
might be fulfilled which was spoken of the Lord by
the prophet, saying, Out of Egypt have
I called my son.
joy

2:16 Then Herod, when he saw that he was **MOCKED** of the wise men, was exceeding **WROTH**, and sent forth, and **SLEW** all the children that were in Bethlehem, and in all the coasts thereof, from two years old and under, according to the time which he had diligently enquired of the wise men.

2:17 Then was fulfilled that which was spoken by Jeremy the prophet, saying,

2:18 In Rama was there a voice heard, **LAMENTATION**, and **WEEPING**, and great **MOURNING**, Rachel weeping for her children, and would not be comforted, because they are not.

2:19 But when Herod was dead, behold, an angel of the Lord appeareth in a dream to Joseph in Egypt,

2:20 Saying, Arise, and take the young child and his mother, and go into the land of Israel: for they are **DEAD** which sought the young child's life.

2:21 And he arose, and took the young child and his mother, and came into the land of Israel.

2:22 But when he heard that Archelaus did reign in Judaea in the room of his father Herod, he was afraid to go thither: notwithstanding, being warned of God in a dream, he turned aside into the parts of Galilee:

2:23 And he came and dwelt in a city called Nazareth: that it might be fulfilled which was spoken by the prophets, He shall be called a Nazarene.

3:1 In those days came John the Baptist, preaching in the wilderness of Judaea,

3:2 And saying, **Repent ye: for the kingdom of heaven is at hand.**

3:3 For this is he that was spoken of by the prophet Esaias, saying, The voice of one crying in the wilderness, **Prepare ye the way of the Lord,** make his paths straight.

3:4 And the same John had his raiment of camel's hair, and a leathern girdle about his loins; and his meat was locusts and wild honey.

Repent

Prepare

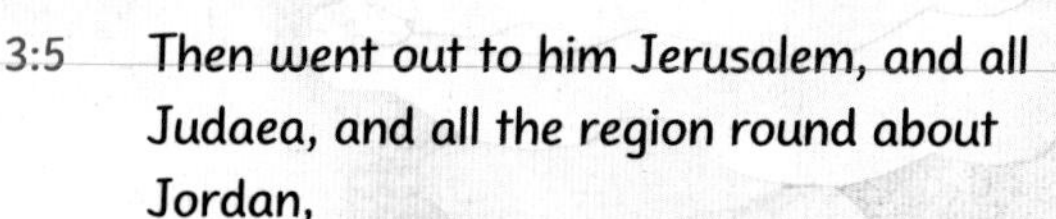

3:5 Then went out to him Jerusalem, and all
Judaea, and all the region round about
Jordan,

3:6 And were baptized of him in Jordan, confessing
their sins.

3:7 But when he saw many of the Pharisees and Sadducees
come to his baptism, he said unto them, O generation of
vipers, who hath warned you to flee from the wrath to
come?

3:8 Bring forth therefore fruits meet for repentance:

3:9 And think not to say within yourselves, We have Abraham
to our father: for I say unto you, that God is able of these
stones to raise up children unto Abraham.

3:10 And now also the axe is laid unto the root of the trees:
therefore every tree which bringeth not forth good fruit is
hewn down, and cast into the fire.

3:11 I indeed baptize you with water unto repentance: but he
that cometh after me is mightier than I, whose shoes I am
not worthy to bear: he shall baptize you with the Holy
Ghost, and with fire:

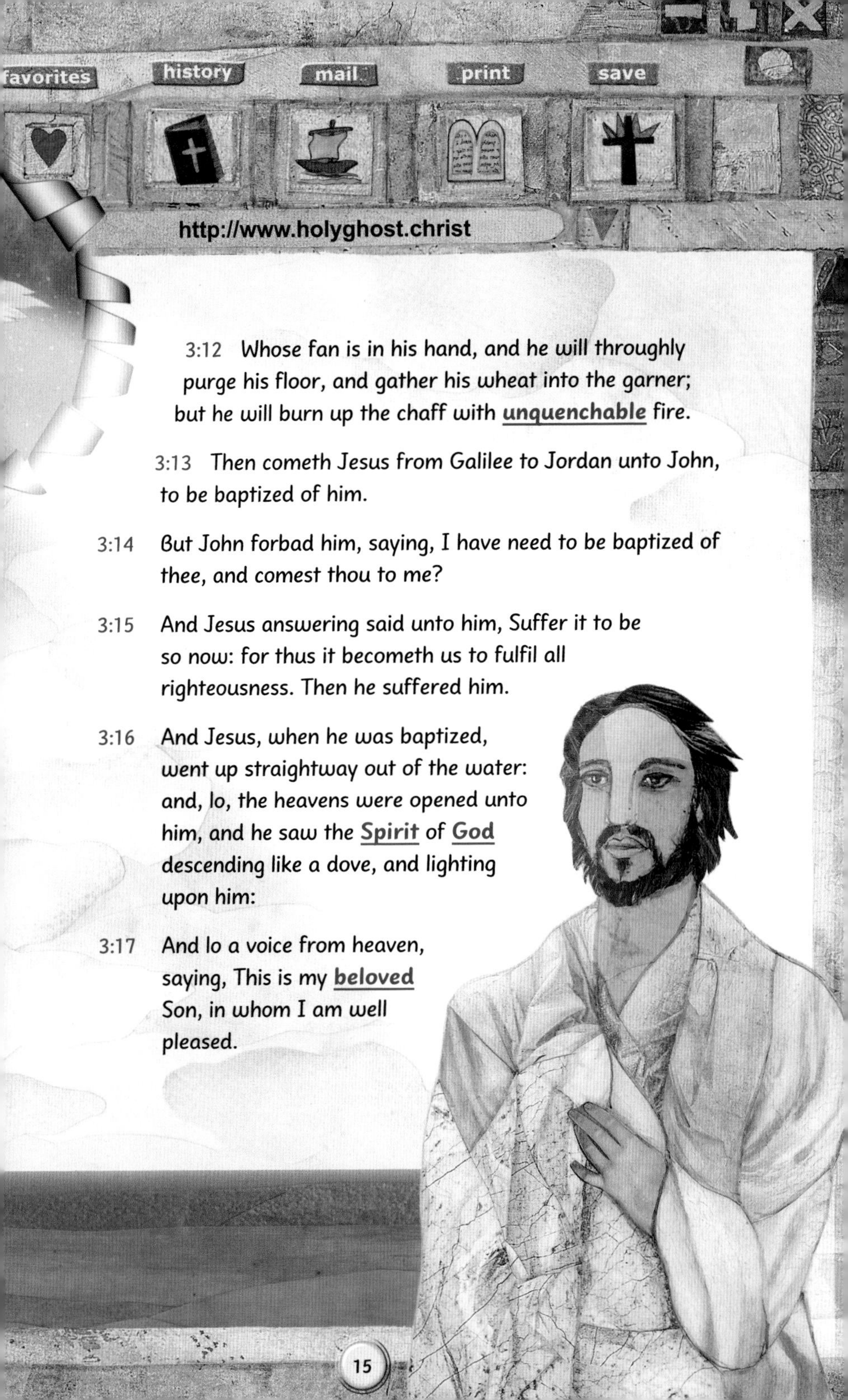

3:12 Whose fan is in his hand, and he will throughly
purge his floor, and gather his wheat into the garner;
but he will burn up the chaff with **unquenchable** fire.

3:13 Then cometh Jesus from Galilee to Jordan unto John,
to be baptized of him.

3:14 But John forbad him, saying, I have need to be baptized of
thee, and comest thou to me?

3:15 And Jesus answering said unto him, Suffer it to be
so now: for thus it becometh us to fulfil all
righteousness. Then he suffered him.

3:16 And Jesus, when he was baptized,
went up straightway out of the water:
and, lo, the heavens were opened unto
him, and he saw the **Spirit** of **God**
descending like a dove, and lighting
upon him:

3:17 And lo a voice from heaven,
saying, This is my **beloved**
Son, in whom I am well
pleased.

4:1 Then was Jesus led up of the spirit into the wilderness to
be tempted of the DEVIL.

4:2 And when he had fasted forty days and forty nights, he
was afterward an hungred.

4:3 And when the TEMPTER came to him, he said, If thou
be the Son of God command that these stones be made
bread.

4:4 But he answered and said, It is written, Man shall not live
by bread alone, but by every word that proceedeth out of
the mouth of God.

4:5 Then the DEVIL taketh him up into the holy city, and
setteth him on a pinnacle of the temple,

4:6 And saith unto him, If thou be the Son of God, cast
thyself down: for it is written, He shall give his angels
charge concerning thee: and in their hands they shall bear
thee up, lest at any time thou dash thy foot against a
stone.

4:7 Jesus said unto him, It is written again, **THOU SHALT NOT TEMPT THE LORD THY GOD.**

4:8 Again, the **DEVIL** taketh him up into an exceeding high mountain, and sheweth him all the kingdoms of the world, and the glory of them;

4:9 And saith unto him, All these things will I give thee, if thou wilt fall down and worship me.

4:10 Then saith Jesus unto him, **GET
THEE HENCE, SATAN** for it is
written, Thou shalt worship
the Lord thy God, and him
only shalt thou serve.

4:11 Then the **DEVIL** leaveth him, and, behold, angels came and ministered unto him.

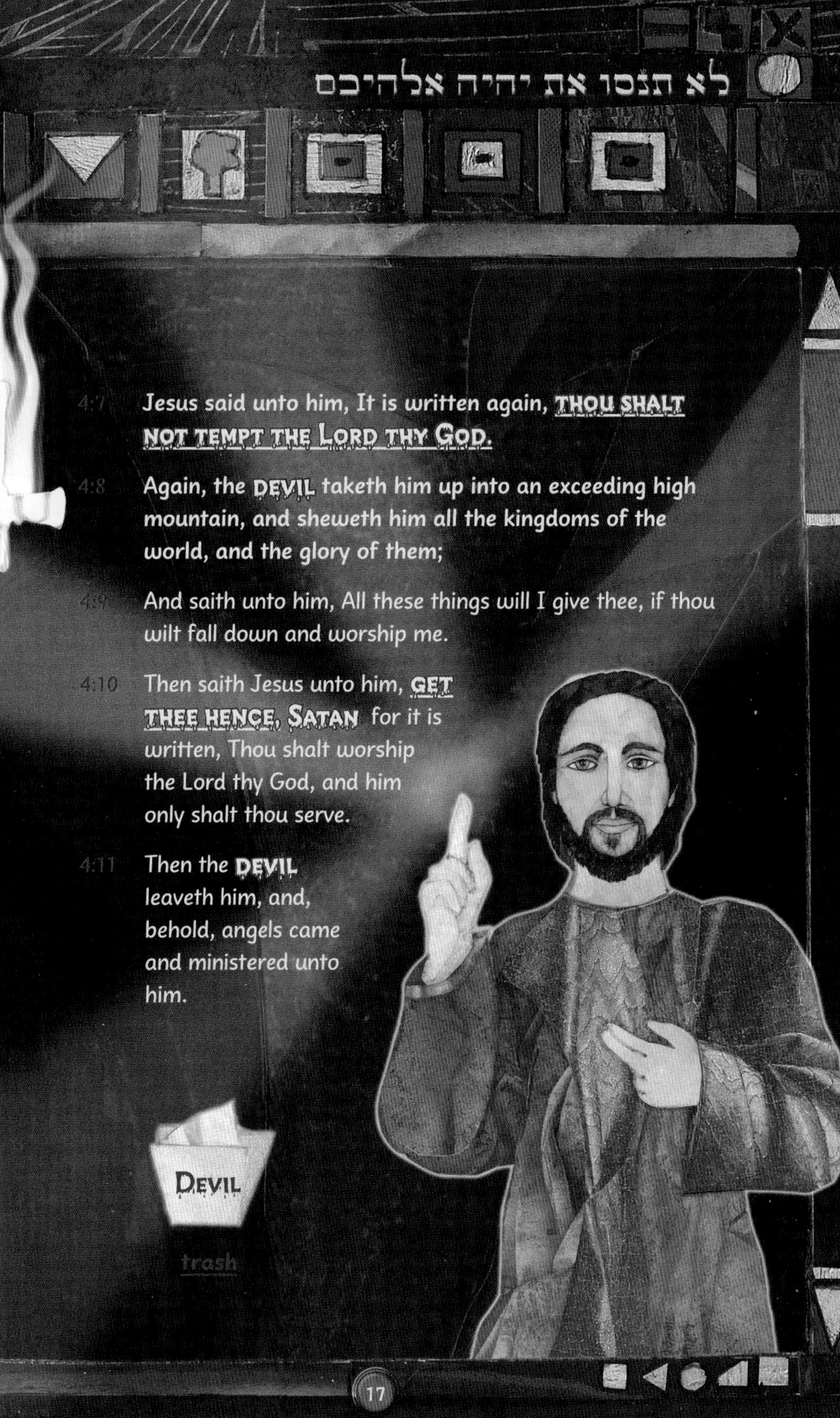

back forward stop grace home search

http://www.fishermen.christ

4:12 Now when Jesus had heard that John was cast into prison, he departed into Galilee;

4:13 And leaving Nazareth, he came and dwelt in Capernaum, which is upon the sea coast, in the borders of Zabulon and Nephthalim:

4:14 That it might be fulfilled which was spoken by Esaias the prophet, saying,

4:15 The land of Zabulon, and the land of Nephthalim, by the way of the sea, beyond Jordan, Galilee of the Gentiles;

4:16 The people which sat in darkness saw great light; and to them which sat in the region and shadow of death light is sprung up.

4:17 From that time Jesus began to preach, and to say, **Repent: for the kingdom of heaven is at hand.**

4:18 And Jesus, walking by the sea of Galilee, saw two brethren, Simon called Peter, and Andrew his brother, casting a net into the sea: for they were fishers.

Peter

John

James

Andrew

4:19 And he saith unto them, **Follow me, and I will make**
you fishers of men.

4:20 And they straightway left their nets, and followed him.

4:21 And going on from thence, he saw other two brethren,
James the son of Zebedee, and John his brother, in a ship
with Zebedee their father, mending their nets; and he
called them.

4:22 And they immediately left the ship and their father, and
followed him.

4:23 And Jesus went about all Galilee, teaching in their
synagogues, and **preaching the gospel** of the kingdom,
and healing all manner of sickness and all manner of
disease among the people.

4:24 And his fame went throughout all Syria: and they brought
unto him all sick people that were taken with divers
diseases and torments, and those which were possessed
with devils, and those which were lunatick, and those that
had the palsy; and **he healed them**.

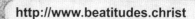

4:25 And there followed him great multitudes of people from Galilee, and from Decapolis, and from Jerusalem, and from Judaea, and from beyond Jordan.

5:1 And seeing the multitudes, he went up into a mountain: and when he was set, his disciples came unto him:

5:2 And he opened his mouth, and taught them, saying,

5:3 ♥ *Blessed* are the poor in spirit: for theirs is the kingdom of heaven.

5:4 ♥ *Blessed* are they that mourn: for they shall be comforted.

5:5 ♥ *Blessed* are the meek: for they shall inherit the earth.

5:6 ♥ *Blessed* are they which do hunger and thirst after righteousness: for they shall be filled.

5:7 ♥ *Blessed* are the merciful: for they shall obtain mercy.

5:8 ♥ *Blessed* are the *pure in heart:* for they shall see God.

5:9 ♥ *Blessed* are the peacemakers: for they shall be called the children of God.

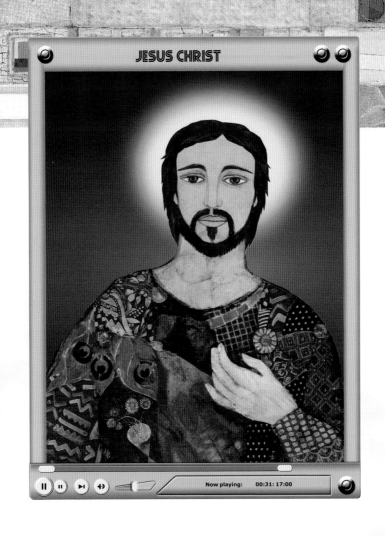

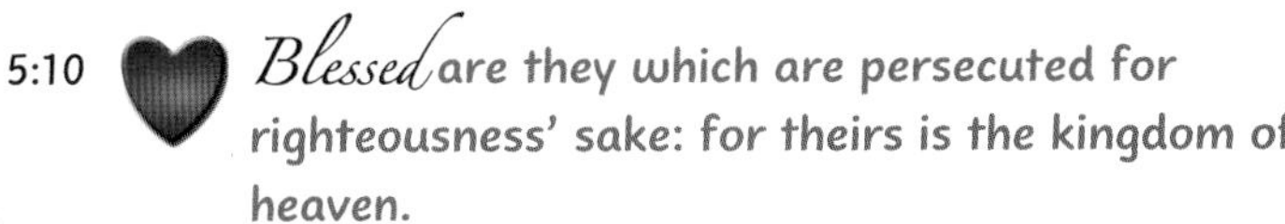

5:10 *Blessed* are they which are persecuted for
righteousness' sake: for theirs is the kingdom of
heaven.

5:11 *Blessed* are ye, when men shall revile you, and
persecute you, and shall say all manner of evil
against you falsely, for my sake.

Matthew 5:14

Ye are the light of the world.

5:12 Rejoice, and be exceeding glad: for great is your reward
in heaven: for so persecuted they the prophets which
were before you.

5:13 Ye are the salt of the earth: but if the salt have lost his
savour, wherewith shall it be salted? it is thenceforth
good for nothing, but to be cast out, and to be
trodden under foot of men.

5:14 Ye are the light of the world. A city that is set
on an hill cannot be hid.

5:15 Neither do men light a candle, and put
it under a bushel, but on a candlestick;
and it giveth light unto all that are in
the house.

5:16 Let your light so shine
before men, that they may
see your good works, and glorify your
Father which is in heaven.

5:17 Think not that I am come to destroy the law, or the
prophets: I am not come to destroy, but to fulfil.

5:18 For verily I say unto you, Till heaven and earth pass,
one jot or one tittle shall in no wise pass from
the law, till all be fulfilled.

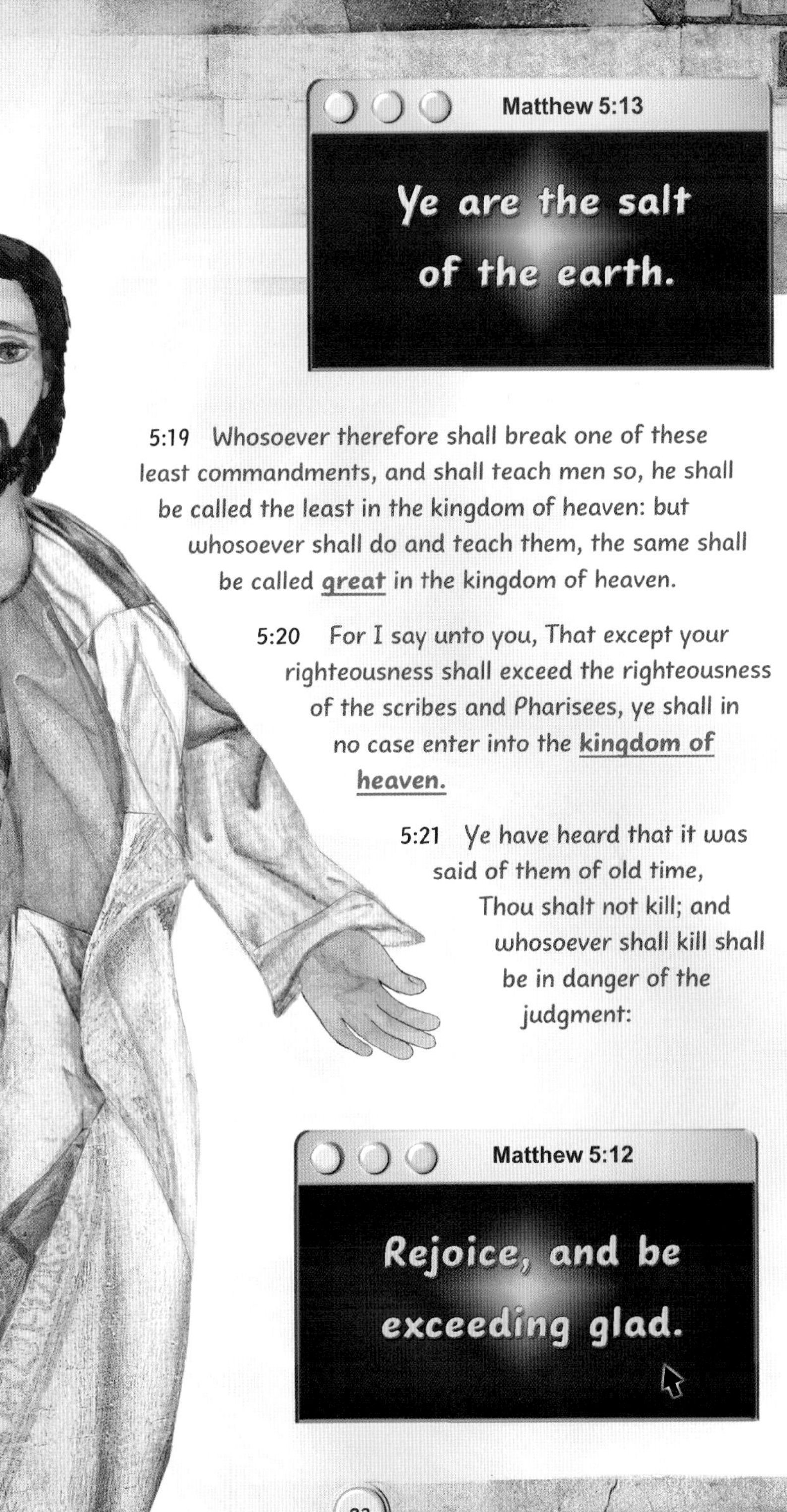

Matthew 5:13

Ye are the salt of the earth.

5:19 Whosoever therefore shall break one of these
least commandments, and shall teach men so, he shall
be called the least in the kingdom of heaven: but
whosoever shall do and teach them, the same shall
be called **great** in the kingdom of heaven.

5:20 For I say unto you, That except your
righteousness shall exceed the righteousness
of the scribes and Pharisees, ye shall in
no case enter into the **kingdom of
heaven.**

5:21 Ye have heard that it was
said of them of old time,
Thou shalt not kill; and
whosoever shall kill shall
be in danger of the
judgment:

Matthew 5:12

Rejoice, and be exceeding glad.

5:22 But I say unto you, That whosoever is angry with
his brother without a cause shall be in danger of the
judgment: and whosoever shall say to his brother, Raca,
shall be in danger of the council: but whosoever shall say,
Thou fool, shall be in danger of hell fire.

5:23 Therefore if thou bring thy gift to the altar, and there
rememberest that thy brother hath ought against thee;

5:24 Leave there thy gift before the altar, and go thy way; first
be reconciled to thy brother, and then come and offer
thy gift.

5:25 **Agree with thine adversary quickly**, whiles
thou art in the way with him; lest at any time the
adversary deliver thee to the judge, and the judge
deliver thee to the officer, and thou be cast into
prison.

5:26 Verily I say unto thee, Thou shalt by no means
come out thence, till thou hast paid the
uttermost farthing.

5:27 Ye have heard that it was said by them of
old time, Thou shalt not commit adultery:

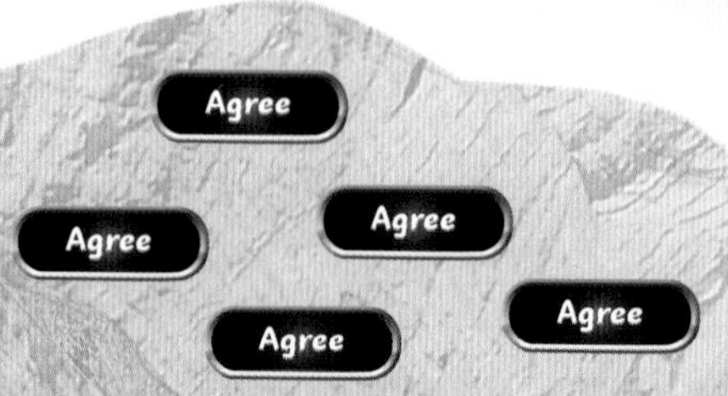

5:28 But I say unto you, That whosoever looketh on a woman to lust after her hath committed adultery with her already in his heart.

5:29 And if thy right eye offend thee, pluck it out, and cast it from thee: for it is profitable for thee that one of thy members should perish, and not that thy whole body should be cast into hell.

5:30 And if thy right hand offend thee, cut it off, and cast it from thee: for it is profitable for thee that one of thy members should perish, and not that thy whole body should be cast into hell.

5:31 It hath been said, Whosoever shall put away his wife, let him give her a writing of divorcement:

5:32 But I say unto you, That whosoever shall put away his wife, saving for the cause of fornication, causeth her to commit adultery: and whosoever shall marry her that is divorced committeth adultery.

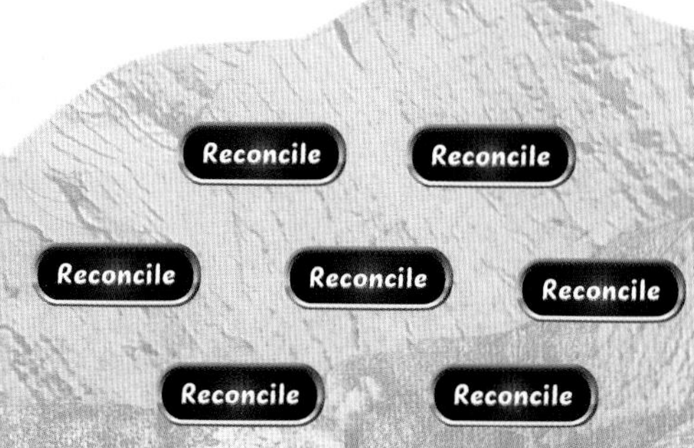

5:33 Again, ye have heard that it hath been said by them of old
time, Thou shalt not forswear thyself, but shalt perform
unto the Lord thine oaths:

5:34 But I say unto you, Swear not at all; neither by heaven; for
it is God's throne:

5:35 Nor by the earth; for it is his footstool: neither
by Jerusalem; for it is the city of the great
King.

5:36 Neither shalt thou swear by thy head,
because thou canst not make one hair
white or black.

5:37 But let your communication be, Yea, yea;
Nay, nay: for whatsoever is more than these
cometh of evil.

5:38 Ye have heard that it hath been said, An eye
for an eye, and a tooth for a tooth:

5:39 But I say unto you, That ye **resist not** evil: but
whosoever shall smite thee on thy right cheek, turn to
him the other also.

5:40 And if any man will sue thee at the law, and take away thy
coat, **let** him have thy cloak also.

n, and pray for them which despitefully use you, and persecute yo

enemies

5:41 And whosoever shall compel thee to go a mile, **go** with him twain.

5:42 **Give** to him that asketh thee, and from him that would borrow of thee turn not thou away.

5:43 Ye have heard that it hath been said, Thou shalt love thy neighbour, and hate thine enemy.

5:44 But I say unto you, **Love your enemies**, bless them that curse you, do good to them that hate you, and pray for them which despitefully use you, and persecute you;

5:45 That ye may be the children of your Father which is in heaven: for he maketh his sun to rise on the evil and on the good, and sendeth rain on the just and on the unjust.

5:46 For if ye **love** them which **love** you, what reward have ye? do not even the publicans the same?

5:47 And if ye **salute** your brethren only, what do ye more than others? do not even the publicans so?

5:48 Be ye therefore perfect, even as your Father which is in heaven is perfect.

ve your enemies, bless them that curse you, do good to them that ha

love

6:1 Take heed that ye do not your alms before men, to be seen of them: otherwise ye have no reward of your Father which is in heaven.

6:2 Therefore when thou doest thine alms, do not sound a trumpet before thee, as the hypocrites do in the synagogues and in the streets, that they may have glory of men. Verily I say unto you, They have their reward.

6:3 But when thou doest alms, **let not thy left hand know what thy right hand doeth:**

6:4 That thine alms may be in secret: and thy Father which seeth in secret himself shall reward thee openly.

6:5 And when thou prayest, thou shalt not be as the hypocrites are: for they love to pray standing in the synagogues and in the corners of the streets, that they may be seen of men. Verily I say unto you, They have their **reward**.

6:6 But thou, when thou prayest, enter into thy closet, and when thou hast shut thy door, **pray** to thy Father which is in secret; and thy Father which seeth in secret shall reward thee openly.

6:7 But when ye **pray**, use not vain repetitions, as the heathen do: for they think that they shall be heard for their much speaking.

6:8 Be not ye therefore like unto them: for your Father knoweth what things ye have need of, before ye ask him.

6:9 After this manner therefore pray ye: Our Father
which art in heaven, Hallowed be thy name.

6:10 Thy kingdom come, Thy will be done in earth, as
it is in heaven.

6:11 <u>Give us</u> this day our daily bread.

6:12 And <u>forgive us</u> our debts, as we forgive our
debtors.

6:13 And lead us not into temptation, but <u>deliver us</u>
from evil: For thine is the kingdom, and
the power, and the glory,
for ever. Amen.

http://www.treasuresoftheheart.christ

6:14 For if ye forgive men their trespasses, your heavenly Father will also forgive you:

6:15 But if ye forgive not men their trespasses, neither will your Father forgive your trespasses.

6:16 Moreover when ye fast, be not, as the hypocrites, of a sad countenance: for they disfigure their faces, that they may appear unto men to fast. Verily I say unto you, They have their reward.

6:17 But thou, when thou fastest, anoint thine head, and wash thy face;

6:18 That thou appear not unto men to fast, but unto thy Father which is in secret: and thy Father, which seeth in secret, shall reward thee openly.

6:19 Lay not up for yourselves treasures upon earth, where moth and rust doth corrupt, and where thieves break through and steal:

6:20 But lay up for yourselves treasures in heaven, where neither moth nor rust doth corrupt, and where thieves do not break through nor steal:

6:21 For where your treasure is, there will your heart be also.

6:22 The light of the body is the eye: if therefore thine eye be single, thy whole body shall be full of light.

the heavenly life

Matthew 6:21

Where your treasure is, there will your heart be also.

6:23 But if thine eye be evil, thy whole body shall be full of darkness. If therefore the light that is in thee be darkness, how great is that darkness!

6:24 No man can serve two masters: for either he will hate the one, and love the other; or else he will hold to the one, and despise the other. Ye cannot serve God and mammon.

6:25 Therefore I say unto you, Take no thought for your life, what ye shall eat, or what ye shall drink; nor yet for your body, what ye shall put on. Is not the life more than meat, and the body than raiment?

6:26 Behold the fowls of the air: for they sow not, neither do they reap, nor gather into barns; yet your heavenly Father feedeth them. Are ye not much better than they?

6:27 Which of you by taking thought can add one cubit unto his stature?

6:28 And why take ye thought for raiment? Consider the lilies of the field, how they grow; they toil not, neither do they spin:

6:29 And yet I say unto you, That even Solomon in all his glory was not arrayed like one of these.

http://www.knockingonheavensdoor.christ

6:30 Wherefore, if God so clothe the grass of the field, which to day is, and to morrow is cast into the oven, shall he not much more clothe you, O ye of little faith?

6:31 Therefore take no thought, saying, What shall we eat? or, What shall we drink? or, Wherewithal shall we be clothed?

6:32 (For after all these things do the Gentiles seek:) for your heavenly Father knoweth that ye have need of all these things.

6:33 But seek ye first the kingdom of God, and his righteousness; and all these things shall be added unto you.

6:34 Take therefore no thought for the morrow: for the morrow shall take thought for the things of itself. Sufficient unto the day is the evil thereof.

7:1 Judge not, that ye be not judged.

7:2 For with what judgment ye judge, ye shall be judged: and with what measure ye mete, it shall be measured to you again.

knock

opening the doors

seek

find

7:3 And why beholdest thou the mote that is in thy
brother's eye, but considerest not the beam that is in
thine own eye?

7:4 Or how wilt thou say to thy brother, Let
me pull out the mote out of thine eye; and,
behold, a beam is in thine own eye?

7:5 Thou hypocrite, first cast out the
beam out of thine own eye; and then
shalt thou see clearly to cast out the
mote out of thy brother's eye.

7:6 Give not that which is holy unto
the dogs, neither cast ye your pearls
before swine, lest they trample them
under their feet, and turn again and
rend you.

7:7 Ask, and it shall be given you;
seek, and ye shall find; knock, and it
shall be opened unto you:

7:8 For every one that asketh receiveth; and he
that seeketh findeth; and to him that knocketh it shall
be opened.

open

7:9 Or what man is there of you, whom if his son ask bread, will he give him a stone?

7:10 Or if he ask a fish, will he give him a serpent?

7:11 If ye then, being evil, know how to give good gifts unto your children, how much more shall your Father which is in heaven give good things to them that ask him?

7:12 Therefore all things whatsoever ye would that men should do to you, do ye even so to them: for this is the law and the prophets.

7:13 Enter ye in at the strait gate: for wide is the gate, and broad is the way, that leadeth to destruction, and many there be which go in thereat:

7:14 Because strait is the gate, and narrow is the way, which leadeth unto life, and few there be that find it.

7:15 **BEWARE OF FALSE PROPHETS**, which come to you in sheep's clothing, but inwardly they are ravening wolves.

7:16 Ye shall know them by their fruits. Do men gather grapes of thorns, or figs of thistles?

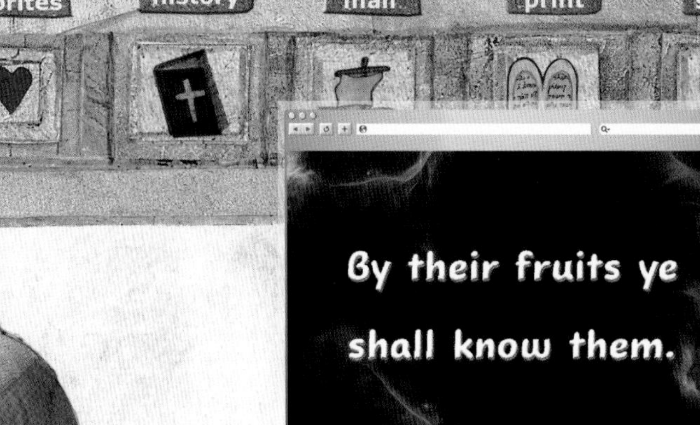
avorites
history
mail
print
save
By their fruits ye
shall know them.

7:17 Even so every good tree bringeth forth good fruit; but a corrupt tree bringeth forth evil fruit.

7:18 A good tree cannot bring forth evil fruit, neither can a corrupt tree bring forth good fruit.

7:19 Every tree that bringeth not forth good fruit is hewn down, and cast into the fire.

7:20 **Wherefore by their fruits ye shall know them.**

7:21 Not every one that saith unto me, Lord, Lord, shall enter into the kingdom of heaven; but he that doeth the will of my Father which is in heaven.

7:22 Many will say to me in that day, Lord, Lord, have we not prophesied in thy name? and in thy name have cast out devils? and in thy name done many wonderful works?

7:23 And then will I profess unto them, I never knew you: depart from me, ye that work iniquity.

7:24 Therefore whosoever heareth these sayings of mine, and doeth them, I will liken him unto a **wise man**, which built his house upon a rock:

back forward stop grace home search

http://www.touch.christ

7:25 And the rain descended, and the floods came,
and the winds blew, and beat upon that house;
and it fell not: for it was **founded upon a rock**.

7:26 And every one that heareth these sayings of mine, and
doeth them not, shall be likened unto a foolish man, which
built his house upon the sand:

7:27 And the rain descended, and the floods came, and the
winds blew, and beat upon that house; and it fell: and
great was the fall of it.

7:28 And it came to pass, when Jesus had ended these sayings,
the people were astonished at his doctrine:

7:29 For he taught them as one having authority, and not as the
scribes.

8:1 When he was come down from the mountain, great
multitudes followed him.

8:2 And, behold, there came a leper and worshipped him,
saying, Lord, if thou wilt, thou canst make me clean.

heal

8:3 And Jesus put forth his hand, and
touched him, saying, I will; be thou clean. And
immediately his leprosy was cleansed.

8:4 And Jesus saith unto him, See thou tell no man;
but go thy way, shew thyself to the priest, and offer the
gift that Moses commanded, for a **testimony** unto them.

8:5 And when Jesus was entered into Capernaum, there came
unto him a centurion, beseeching him,

8:6 And saying, Lord, my servant lieth at home sick of the
palsy, grievously tormented.

8:7 And Jesus saith unto him, **I will come and heal him.**

8:8 The centurion answered and said, Lord, I am not worthy
that thou shouldest come under my roof: but speak the
word only, and my servant shall be **healed**.

8:9 For I am a man under authority, having soldiers under me:
and I say to this man, Go, and he goeth; and to another,
Come, and he cometh; and to my servant, Do this, and he
doeth it.

8:10 When Jesus heard it, he marvelled, and said to them that followed, Verily I say unto you, I have not found so great **faith**, no, not in Israel.

8:11 And I say unto you, That many shall come from the east and west, and shall sit down with Abraham, and Isaac, and Jacob, in the kingdom of heaven.

8:12 But the children of the kingdom shall be cast out into outer darkness: there shall be weeping and gnashing of teeth.

8:13 And Jesus said unto the centurion, Go thy way; and as thou hast **believed**, so be it done unto thee. And his servant was healed in the selfsame hour.

8:14 And when Jesus was come into Peter's house, he saw his wife's mother laid, and sick of a fever.

8:15 And he **touched** her hand, and the fever left her: and she arose, and ministered unto them.

8:16 When the even was come, they brought unto him many that were possessed with devils: and he cast out the spirits with his word, and **healed** all that were sick:

8:17 That it might be fulfilled which was spoken by Esaias the prophet, saying, Himself took our infirmities, and bare our sicknesses.

8:18 Now when Jesus saw great multitudes about him, he gave commandment to depart unto the other side.

8:19 And a certain scribe came, and said unto him, Master, I
will follow thee whithersoever thou goest.

8:20 And Jesus saith unto him, The foxes have holes, and the
birds of the air have nests; but the Son of man hath not
where to lay his head.

8:21 And another of his disciples said unto him, Lord, suffer me
first to go and bury my father.

8:22 But Jesus said unto him, Follow me; and **LET THE DEAD
BURY THEIR DEAD.**

touch

heal

8:23 And when he was entered into a ship, his disciples
followed him.

8:24 And, behold, there arose a great tempest in the
sea, insomuch that the ship was covered with the
waves: but he was asleep.

8:25 And his disciples came to him, and awoke him,
saying, Lord save us: we perish.

confess
chat
pray
Christ
Lord, save us!
SAVE

The Calming of the Storm

8:26 And he saith unto them, Why are ye fearful, O ye of little
faith? Then he arose, and rebuked the winds and the sea;
and there was a great calm.

8:27 But the men marvelled, saying, What manner of man is
this, that even the winds and the sea obey him!

8:28 And when he was come to the other side into the country of the Gergesenes, there met him two possessed with devils, coming out of the tombs, exceeding fierce, so that no man might pass by that way.

8:29 And, behold, they cried out, saying, What have we to do with thee, Jesus, thou Son of God? art thou come hither to torment us before the time?

8:30 And there was a good way off from them an herd of many swine feeding.

8:31 So the devils besought him, saying, If thou cast us out, suffer us to go away into the herd of swine.

8:32 And he said unto them, Go. And when they were come out, they went into the herd of swine: and, behold, the whole herd of swine ran violently down a steep place into the sea, and perished in the waters.

8:33 And they that kept them fled, and went their ways into the city, and told every thing, and what was befallen to the possessed of the devils.

8:34 And, behold, the whole city came out to meet Jesus: and when they saw him, they besought him that he would depart out of their coasts.

9:1 And he entered into a ship, and passed over, and came into his own city.

9:2 And, behold, they brought to him a man sick of the palsy,
lying on a bed: and Jesus seeing their faith said unto the
sick of the palsy; **Son, be of good cheer; thy sins be**
forgiven thee.

9:3 And, behold, certain of the scribes said within themselves,
This man blasphemeth.

9:4 And Jesus knowing their thoughts said, Wherefore think ye
evil in your hearts?

9:5 For whether is easier, to say, Thy sins be forgiven thee; or
to say, **Arise**, and **walk**?

9:6 But that ye may know that the Son of man hath **power**
on earth to **forgive** sins, (then saith he to the sick of the
palsy,) Arise, take up thy bed, and go unto thine house.

9:7 And he arose, and departed to his house.

arise

walk

9:8 But when the multitudes saw it, they marvelled, and glorified God, which had given such power unto men.

9:9 And as Jesus passed forth from thence, he saw a man, named Matthew, sitting at the receipt of custom: and he saith unto him, Follow me. And he arose, and followed him.

9:10 And it came to pass, as Jesus sat at meat in the house, behold, many publicans and sinners came and sat down with him and his disciples.

9:11 And when the Pharisees saw it, they said unto his disciples, Why eateth your Master with publicans and sinners?

9:12 But when Jesus heard that, he said unto them, They that be whole need not a physician, but they that are sick.

9:13 But go ye and learn what that meaneth,
I will have mercy, and not sacrifice: for I am not come to call the righteous, but sinners to repentance.

9:14 Then came to him the disciples of John, saying, Why do we and the Pharisees fast oft, but thy disciples fast not?

9:15 And Jesus said unto them, Can the children of the bridechamber mourn, as long as the bridegroom is with them? but the days will come, when the bridegroom shall be taken from them, and then shall they fast.

9:16 No man putteth a piece of new cloth unto an old garment, for that which is put in to fill it up taketh from the garment, and the rent is made worse.

9:17 Neither do men put new wine into old bottles: else the bottles break, and the wine runneth out, and the bottles perish: but they put **new wine** into **new bottles**, and both are preserved.

9:18 While he spake these things unto them, behold, there came a certain ruler, and worshipped him, saying, My daughter is even now dead: but come and lay thy hand upon her, and she shall live.

9:19 And Jesus arose, and followed him, and so did his disciples.

9:20 And, behold, a woman, which was diseased with an issue
of blood twelve years, came behind him, and touched the
hem of his garment:

9:21 For she said within herself, If I may but touch his garment,
I shall be whole.

9:22 But Jesus turned him about, and when he saw her, he
said, Daughter, be of good **comfort**; thy **faith** hath made
thee whole. And the woman was made whole from that
hour.

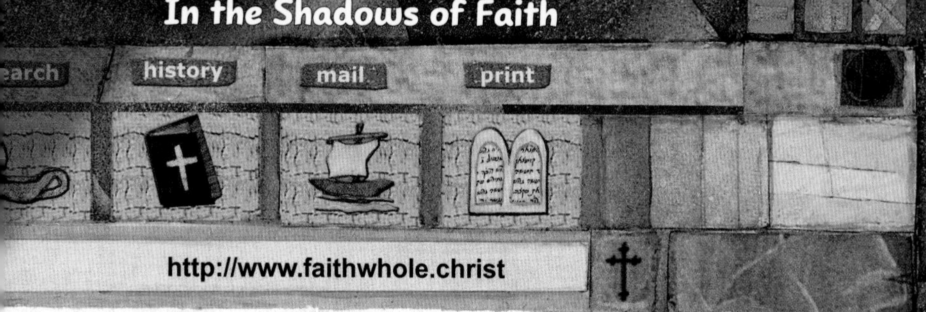

9:23 And when Jesus came into the ruler's house, and saw the minstrels and the people making a noise,

9:24 He said unto them, Give place: for the maid is not dead, but sleepeth. And they laughed him to scorn.

9:25 But when the people were put forth, he went in, and took her by the hand, and the maid arose.

9:26 And the fame hereof went abroad into all that land.

back forward stop refresh home favorites

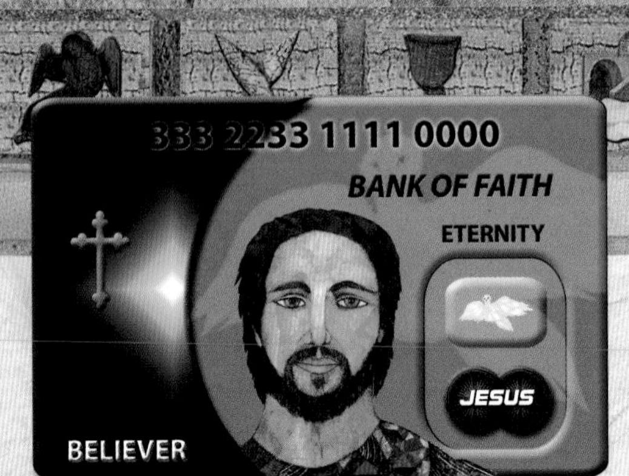

faith card click here

9:27 And when Jesus departed thence, two blind men followed him, crying, and saying, Thou son of David, have mercy on us.

9:28 And when he was come into the house, the blind men came to him: and Jesus saith unto them, Believe ye that I am able to do this? They said unto him, Yea, Lord.

9:29 Then touched he their eyes, saying, According to your **faith** be it unto you.

9:30 And their **eyes** were **opened**; and Jesus straitly charged them, saying, See that no man know it.

9:31 But they, when they were departed, spread abroad his fame in all that country.

9:32 As they went out, behold, they brought to him a dumb man possessed with a devil.

9:33 And when the devil was cast out, the dumb spake: and the multitudes marvelled, saying, It was never so seen in Israel.

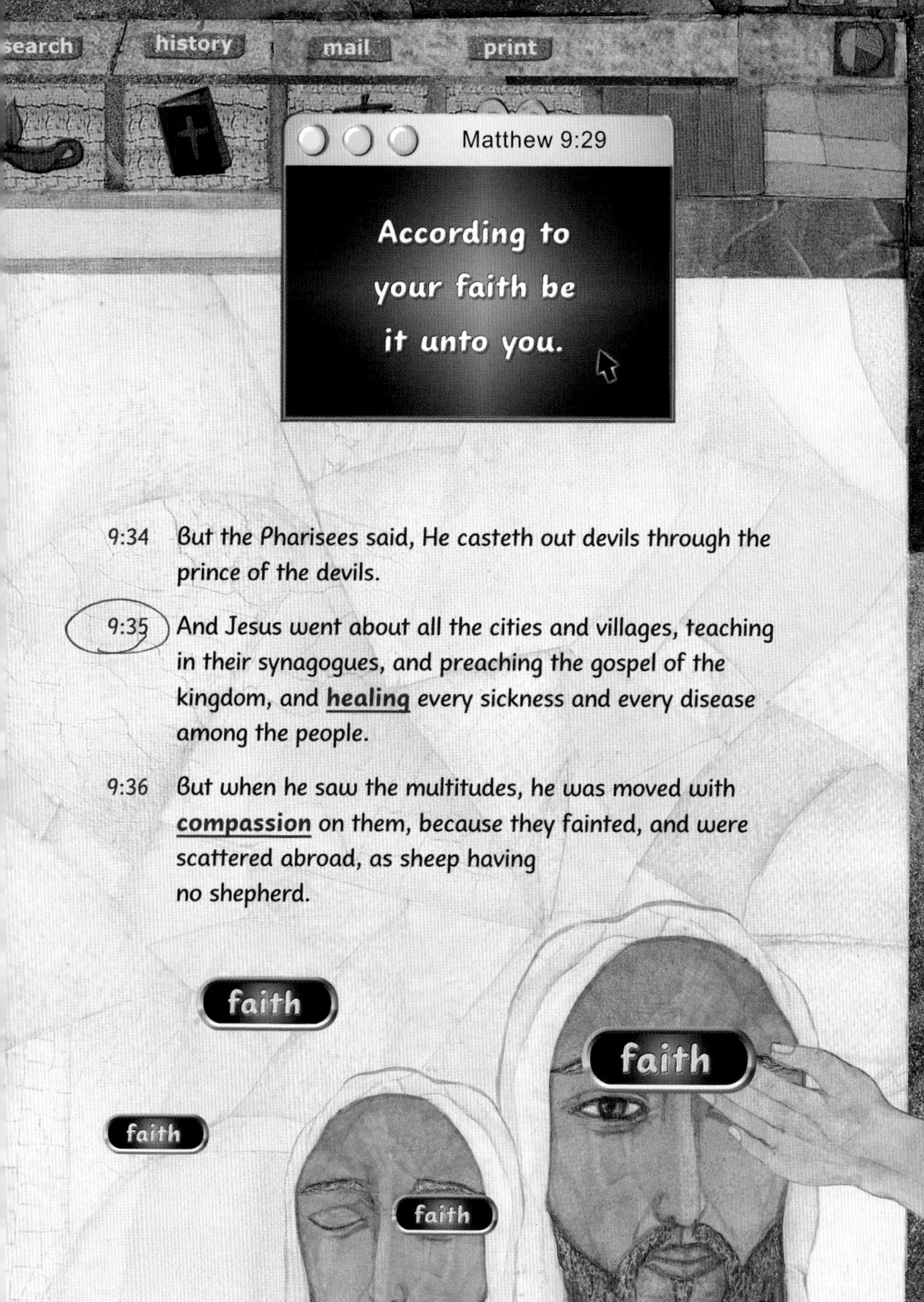

9:34 But the Pharisees said, He casteth out devils through the prince of the devils.

9:35 And Jesus went about all the cities and villages, teaching in their synagogues, and preaching the gospel of the kingdom, and **healing** every sickness and every disease among the people.

9:36 But when he saw the multitudes, he was moved with **compassion** on them, because they fainted, and were scattered abroad, as sheep having no shepherd.

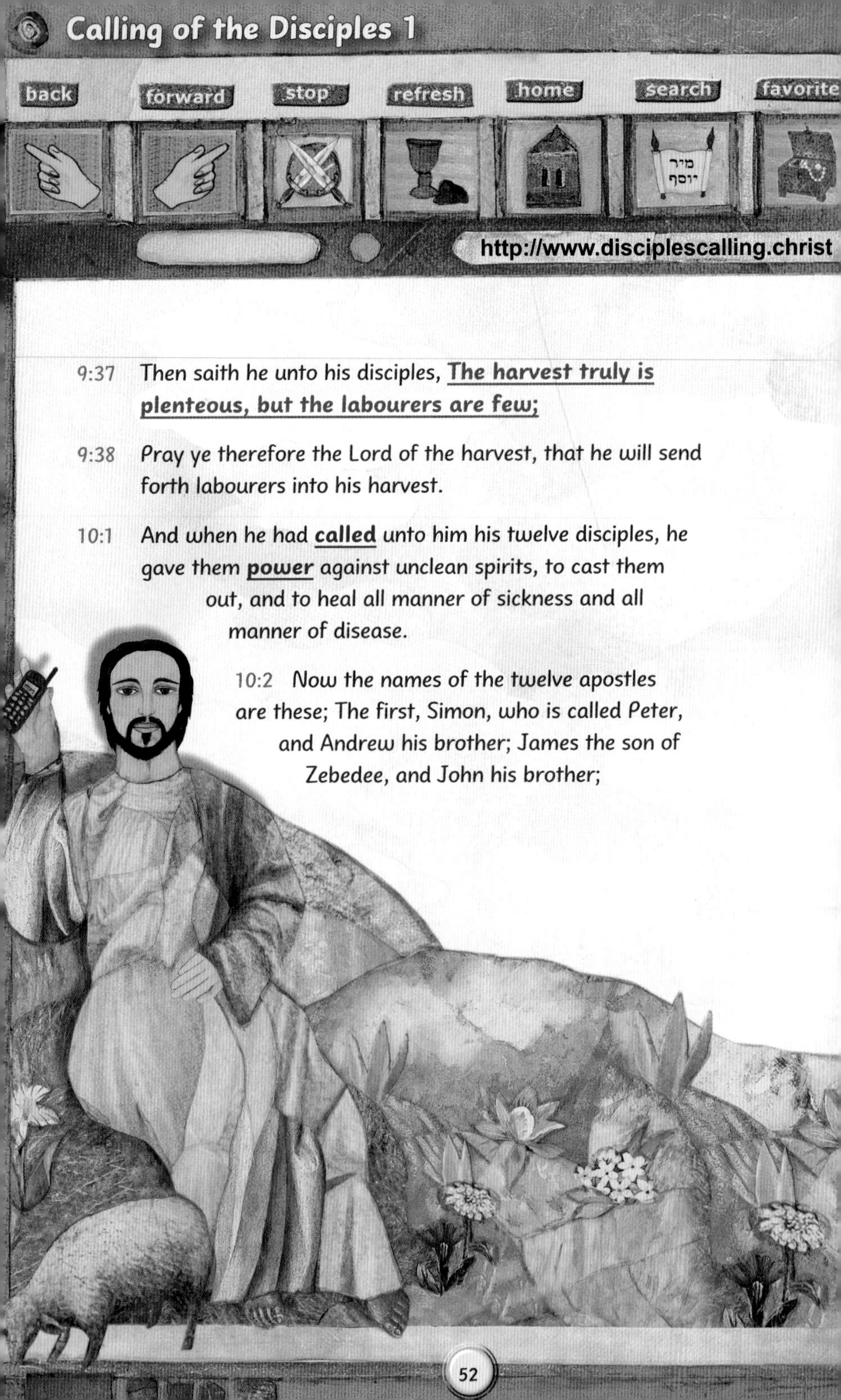

9:37 Then saith he unto his disciples, **The harvest truly is plenteous, but the labourers are few;**

9:38 Pray ye therefore the Lord of the harvest, that he will send forth labourers into his harvest.

10:1 And when he had **called** unto him his twelve disciples, he gave them **power** against unclean spirits, to cast them out, and to heal all manner of sickness and all manner of disease.

10:2 Now the names of the twelve apostles are these; The first, Simon, who is called Peter, and Andrew his brother; James the son of Zebedee, and John his brother;

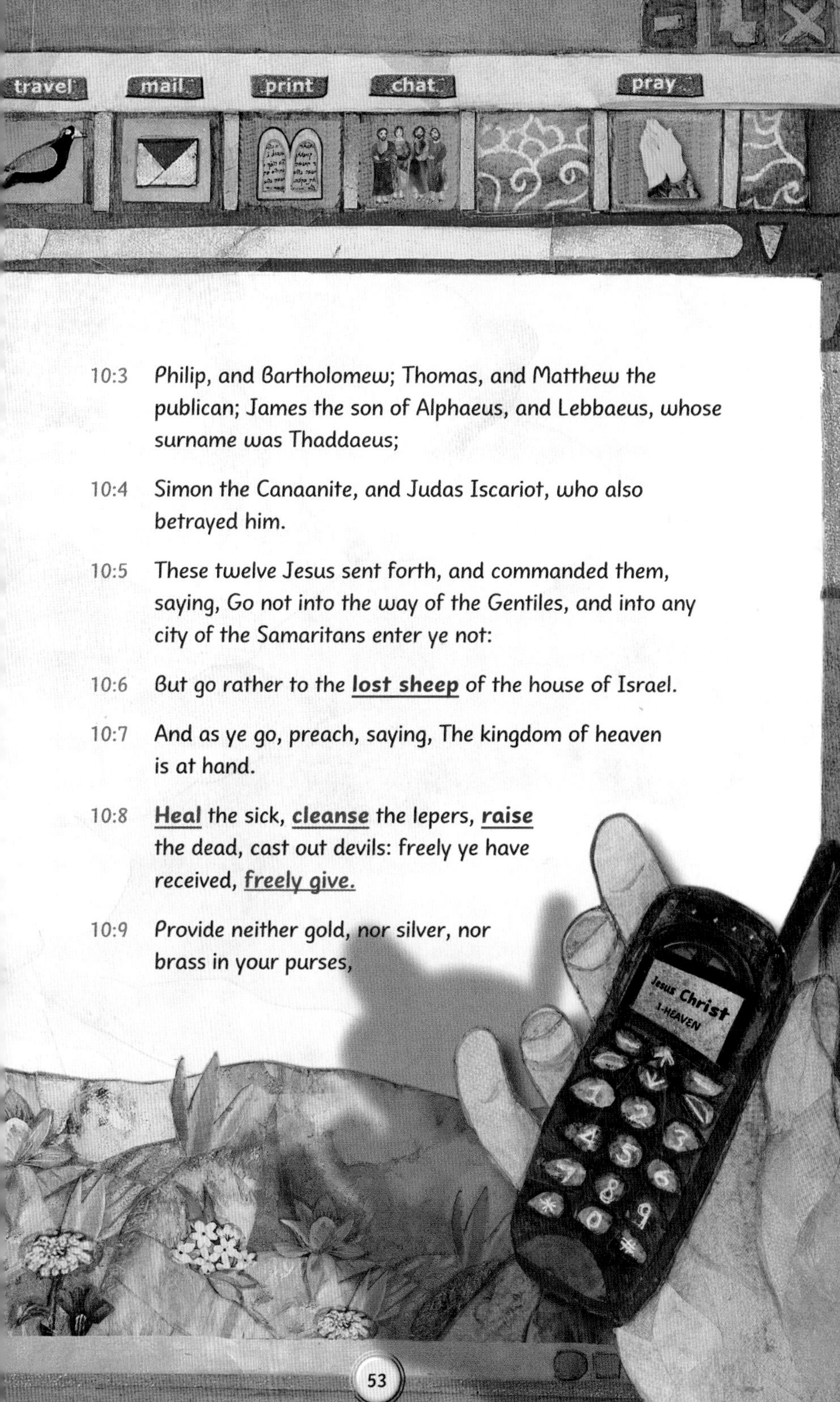

10:3 Philip, and Bartholomew; Thomas, and Matthew the publican; James the son of Alphaeus, and Lebbaeus, whose surname was Thaddaeus;

10:4 Simon the Canaanite, and Judas Iscariot, who also betrayed him.

10:5 These twelve Jesus sent forth, and commanded them, saying, Go not into the way of the Gentiles, and into any city of the Samaritans enter ye not:

10:6 But go rather to the **lost sheep** of the house of Israel.

10:7 And as ye go, preach, saying, The kingdom of heaven is at hand.

10:8 **Heal** the sick, **cleanse** the lepers, **raise** the dead, cast out devils: freely ye have received, **freely give.**

10:9 Provide neither gold, nor silver, nor brass in your purses,

10:10 Nor scrip for your journey, neither two coats, neither shoes, nor yet staves: for the workman is worthy of his meat.

10:11 And into whatsoever city or town ye shall enter, enquire who in it is worthy; and there abide till ye go thence.

10:12 And when ye come into an house, salute it.

10:13 And if the house be worthy, let your peace come upon it: but if it be not worthy, let your peace return to you.

10:14 And whosoever shall not receive you, nor hear your words, when ye depart out of that house or city, **shake off the dust of your feet.**

10:15 Verily I say unto you, It shall be more tolerable for the land of Sodom and Gomorrha in the day of judgment, than for that city.

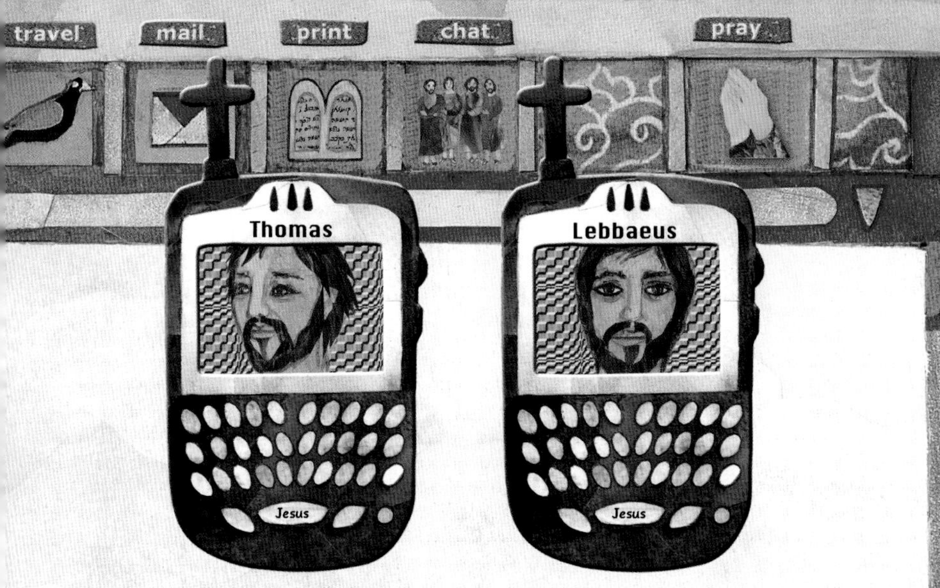

10:16 Behold, I send you forth as sheep in the midst of wolves: **be ye therefore wise as SERPENTS, and harmless as doves.**

10:17 But **BEWARE OF MEN**: for they will deliver you up to the councils, and they will scourge you in their synagogues;

10:18 And ye shall be brought before governors and kings for my sake, for a testimony against them and the Gentiles.

10:19 But when they deliver you up, take no thought how or what ye shall speak: for it shall be given you in that same hour what ye shall speak.

10:19 **For it is not ye that speak, but the Spirit of your Father which speaketh in you.**

10:21 And the brother shall deliver up the brother to death, and the father the child: and the children shall rise up against their parents, and cause them to be put to death.

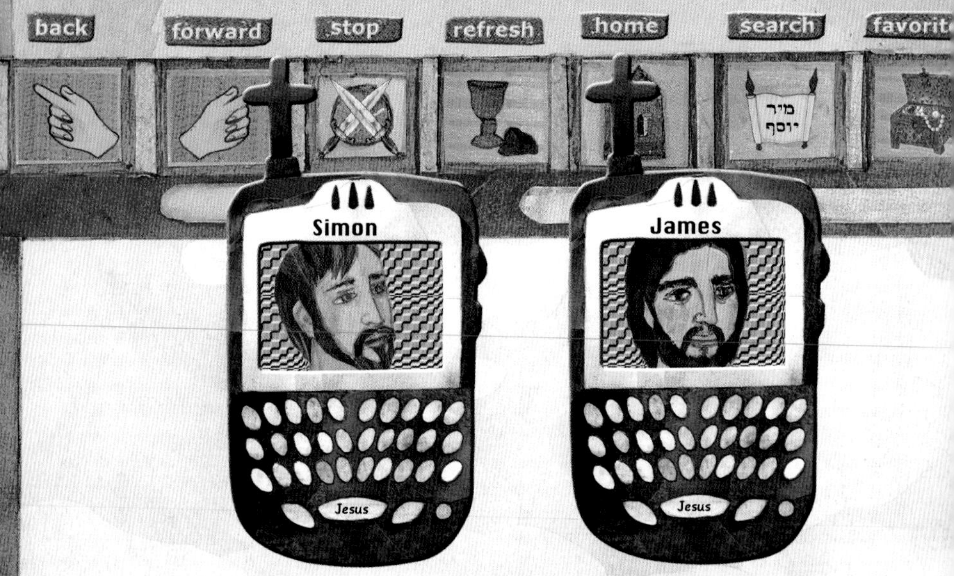

10:22 And ye shall be **HATED** of all men for my name's sake:
but **he that endureth to the end shall be saved.**

10:23 But when they persecute you in this city, flee ye into
another: for verily I say unto you, Ye shall not have gone
over the cities of Israel, till the Son of man be come.

10:24 The disciple is not above his master, nor the servant above
his lord.

10:25 It is enough for the disciple that he be as his master, and
the servant as his lord. If they have called the master of
the house Beelzebub, how much more shall they call them
of his household?

10:26 **Fear them not** therefore: for there is nothing covered,
that shall not be revealed; and hid, that shall not be
known.

10:27 What I tell you in **DARKNESS**, that speak ye in light:
and what ye hear in the ear, that preach ye upon the
housetops.

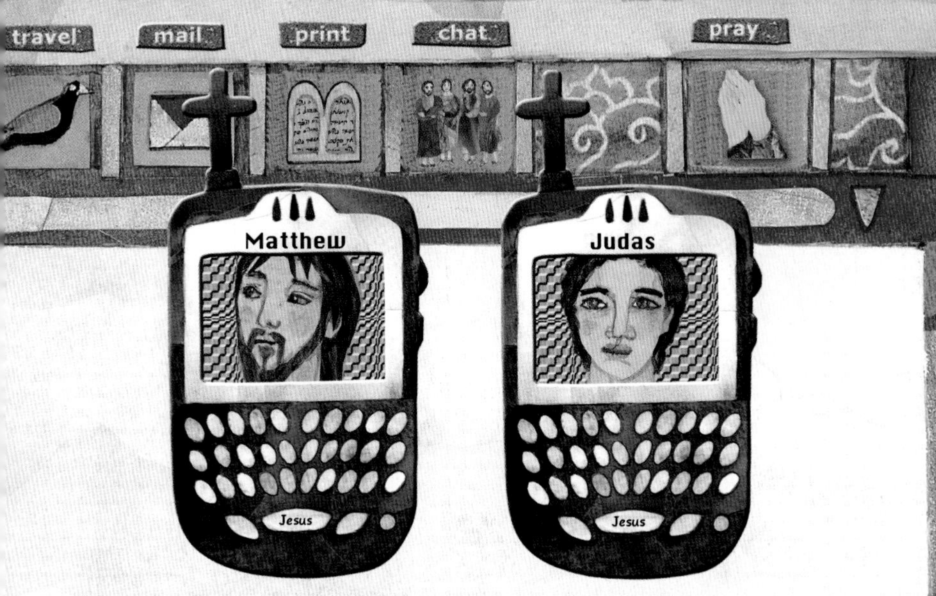

10:28 And fear not them which kill the body, but are not able to kill the soul: but rather **FEAR** him which is able to destroy both soul and body in hell.

10:29 Are not two sparrows sold for a farthing? and one of them shall not fall on the ground without your Father.

10:30 But the very hairs of your head are all numbered.

10:31 Fear ye not therefore, ye are of more value than many sparrows.

10:32 Whosoever therefore shall confess me before men, him will I confess also before my Father which is in heaven.

10:33 But whosoever shall **DENY** me before men, him will I also **DENY** before my Father which is in heaven.

10:34 Think not that I am come to send peace on earth: I came not to send peace, but a sword.

10:35 For I am come to set a man at variance against his father, and the daughter against her mother, and the daughter in law against her mother in law.

10:36 And a man's foes shall be they of his own household.

10:37 He that loveth father or mother more than me is not worthy of me: and he that loveth son or daughter more than me is not worthy of me.

10:38 And he that taketh not his **cross**, and followeth after me, is not **worthy** of me.

10:39 He that findeth his life shall lose it: and **he that loseth his life for my sake shall find it.**

10:40 He that receiveth you receiveth me, and he that receiveth me receiveth him that sent me.

10:41 He that receiveth a prophet in the name of a prophet shall receive a prophet's **reward**; and he that receiveth a righteous man in the name of a righteous man shall receive a righteous man's **reward**.

10:42 And whosoever shall give to drink unto one of these little ones a cup of cold water only in the name of a disciple, verily I say unto you, he shall in no wise lose his **reward**.

11:1 And it came to pass, when Jesus had made an end of commanding his twelve disciples, he departed thence to teach and to preach in their cities.

11:2 Now when John had heard in the prison the works of Christ, he sent two of his disciples,

11:3 And said unto him, Art thou he that should come, or do we look for another?

11:4 Jesus answered and said unto them, Go and shew John again those things which ye do hear and see:

11:5 The blind receive their sight, and the lame walk, the lepers are **cleansed**, and the deaf hear, the dead are raised up, and the poor have the gospel preached to them.

11:6 And **blessed** is he, whosoever shall not be offended in me.

11:7 And as they departed, Jesus began to say unto the multitudes concerning John, What went ye out into the wilderness to see? A reed shaken with the wind?

11:8 But what went ye out for to see? A man clothed in soft raiment? behold, they that wear soft clothing are in kings' houses.

11:9 But what went ye out for to see? A prophet? yea, I say unto you, and more than a prophet.

11:10 For this is he, of whom it is written, Behold, I send my messenger before thy face, which shall prepare thy way before thee.

11:11 Verily I say unto you, Among them that are born of women there hath not risen a greater than John the Baptist: notwithstanding he that is least in the kingdom of heaven is greater than he.

11:12 And from the days of John the Baptist until now the kingdom of heaven suffereth violence, and the violent take it by force.

11:13 For all the prophets and the law prophesied until John.

11:14 And if ye will receive it, this is Elias, which was for to come.

11:15 **He that hath ears to hear, let him hear.**

11:16 But whereunto shall I liken this generation? It is like unto children sitting in the markets, and calling unto their fellows,

11:17 And saying, We have piped unto you, and ye have not danced; we have mourned unto you, and ye have not lamented.

11:18 For John came neither eating nor drinking, and they say, He hath a devil.

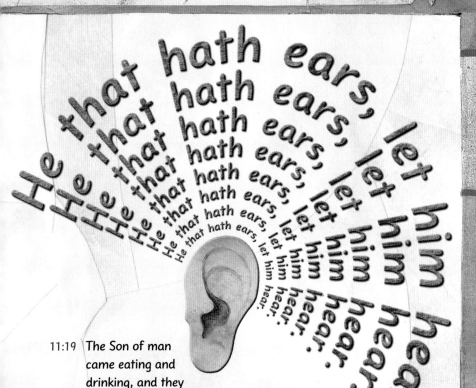

He that hath ears, let him hear.
He that hath ears, let him hear.
He that hath ears, let him hear.
He that hath ears, let him hear.
He that hath ears, let him hear.
He that hath ears, let him hear.
He that hath ears, let him hear.
He that hath ears, let him hear.

11:19 The Son of man
came eating and
drinking, and they
say, Behold a man gluttonous, and a
winebibber, a friend of publicans and sinners.
But wisdom is justified of her children.

11:20 Then began he to upbraid the cities wherein most of his
mighty works were done, because they repented not:

11:21 Woe unto thee, Chorazin! woe unto thee, Bethsaida! for if
the mighty works, which were done in you, had been done
in Tyre and Sidon, they would have repented long ago in
sackcloth and ashes.

11:22 But I say unto you, It shall be more tolerable for Tyre and Sidon at the day of judgment, than for you.

11:23 And thou, Capernaum, which art exalted unto heaven, shalt be brought down to hell: for if the mighty works, which have been done in thee, had been done in Sodom, it would have remained until this day.

11:24 But I say unto you, That it shall be more tolerable for the land of Sodom in the day of judgment, than for thee.

11:25 At that time Jesus answered and said, I thank thee, O Father, Lord of heaven and earth, because thou hast hid these things from the wise and prudent, and hast revealed them unto babes.

easy

My Burden Is Light

11:26 Even so, Father: for so it seemed good in thy sight.

11:27 All things are delivered unto me of my Father: and no man knoweth the Son, but the Father; neither knoweth any man the Father, save the Son, and he to whomsoever the Son will reveal him.

11:28 Come unto me, all ye that labour and are heavy laden, and I will give you **rest**.

11:29 Take my yoke upon you, and learn of me; for I am meek and lowly in **heart**: and ye shall find **rest** unto your souls.

11:30 For my yoke is **easy**, and my burden is **light**.

light

back forward stop refresh home favorites

http://www.sabbath.christ

12:1 At that time Jesus went on the sabbath day through the corn; and his disciples were an **hungred**, and began to pluk the ears of corn and to **eat**.

12:2 But when the Pharisees saw it, they said unto him, Behold, thy disciples do that which is not **lawful** to do upon the sabbath day.

12:3 But he said unto them, Have ye not read what David did, when he was an hungred, and they that were with him;

12:4 How he entered into the house of **God**, and did eat the shewbread, which was not lawful for him to eat, neither for them which were with him, but only for the priests?

12:5 Or have ye not read in the law, how that on the sabbath days the priests in the temple profane the sabbath, and are blameless?

12:6 But I say unto you, That in this place is one greater than the temple.

12:7 But if ye had known what this meaneth, I will have **mercy**, and not sacrifice, ye would not have condemned the **guiltless**.

12:8 For the Son of **man** is **Lord** even of the **sabbath** day.

lawful

mercy

guiltless

מלך

שׁבת

12:9 And when he was departed thence, he went into their synagogue:

12:10 And, behold, there was a man which had his hand withered. And they asked him, saying, Is it lawful to heal on the sabbath days? that they might accuse him.

12:11 And he said unto them, What man shall there be among you, that shall have one sheep, and if it fall into a pit on the sabbath day, will he not lay hold on it, and lift it out?

12:12 How much then is a man better than a sheep? Wherefore it is lawful to do well on the sabbath days.

12:13 Then saith he to the man, Stretch forth thine hand. And he stretched it forth; and it was restored whole, like as the other.

12:14 Then the Pharisees went out, and held a council against him, how they might destroy him.

12:15 But when Jesus knew it, he withdrew himself from thence: and great multitudes followed him, and he healed them all;

12:16 And charged them that they should not make him known:

Christ

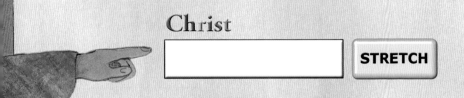

STRETCH

trust card click here

12:17 That it might be fulfilled which was spoken by Esaias the prophet, saying,

12:18 Behold my servant, whom I have chosen; my beloved, in whom my soul is well pleased: I will put my spirit upon him, and he shall shew judgment to the Gentiles.

12:19 He shall not strive, nor cry; neither shall any man hear his voice in the streets.

12:20 A bruised reed shall he not break, and smoking flax shall he not quench, till he send forth judgment unto victory.

12:21 And in his name shall the Gentiles **trust**.

12:22 Then was brought unto him one possessed with a devil, blind, and dumb: and he healed him, insomuch that the blind and dumb both spake and saw.

12:23 And all the people were amazed, and said, Is not this the son of David?

Christ

TRUST

back forward stop refresh home search favorite

faith	† f
compassion	† c
charity	^† c
love	>
hope	† h
kindness	† k

God	† G
family	^† F
friends	^^† F
neighbors	† n

http://www.forgiveness.christ

12:24 But when the Pharisees heard it, they said, This fellow
doth not cast out devils, but by Beelzebub the prince of the
devils.

12:25 And Jesus knew their thoughts, and said unto them, Every
kingdom divided against itself is brought to desolation; and
<u>every city or house divided against itself shall not
stand:</u>

12:26 And if Satan cast out Satan, he is divided against himself;
how shall then his kingdom stand?

12:27 And if I by Beelzebub cast out devils, by whom do your
children cast them out? therefore they shall be your judges.

12:28 But if I cast out devils by the Spirit of God, then the
kingdom of God is come unto you.

12:29 Or else how can one enter into a strong man's house, and
spoil his goods, except he first bind the strong man? and
then he will spoil his house.

12:30 He that is not with me is against me; and he that gathereth
not with me scattereth abroad.

12:31 Wherefore I say unto you, All manner of sin and blasphemy shall be forgiven unto men: but the blasphemy against the Holy Ghost shall not be forgiven unto men.

12:32 And whosoever speaketh a word against the Son of man, it shall be forgiven him: but whosoever speaketh against the Holy Ghost, it shall not be forgiven him, neither in this world, neither in the world to come.

12:33 Either make the tree good, and his fruit good; or else make the tree corrupt, and his fruit corrupt: for the tree is known by his fruit.

12:34 O generation of vipers, how can ye, being evil, speak good things? for out of the abundance of the heart the mouth speaketh.

12:35 A good man out of the good treasure of the heart bringeth forth good things: and an evil man out of the evil treasure bringeth forth evil things.

12:36 But I say unto you, That every idle word that men shall speak, they shall give account thereof in the day of judgment.

12:37 For by thy words thou shalt be justified, and by thy words thou shalt be condemned.

forgiveness

12:38 Then certain of the scribes and of the Pharisees answered, saying, Master, we would see a sign from thee.

12:39 But he answered and said unto them, An evil and adulterous generation seeketh after a sign; and there shall no sign be given to it, but the sign of the prophet Jonas:

12:40 For as Jonas was three days and three nights in the whale's belly; so shall the Son of man be three days and three nights in the heart of the earth.

12:41 The men of Nineveh shall rise in judgment with this generation, and shall condemn it: because they repented at the preaching of Jonas; and, behold, a greater than Jonas is here.

12:42 The queen of the south shall rise up in the judgment with this generation, and shall condemn it: for she came from the uttermost parts of the earth to hear the wisdom of Solomon; and, behold, a greater than Solomon is here.

12:43 When the unclean spirit is gone out of a man, he walketh through dry places, seeking rest, and findeth none.

12:44 Then he saith, I will return into my house from whence I came out; and when he is come, he findeth it empty, swept, and garnished.

12:45 Then goeth he, and taketh with himself seven other spirits more wicked than himself, and they enter in and dwell there: and the last state of that man is worse than the first. Even so shall it be also unto this wicked generation.

12:46 While he yet talked to the people, behold, his mother and his brethren stood without, desiring to speak with him.

12:47 Then one said unto him, Behold, thy mother and thy brethren stand without, desiring to speak with thee.

12:48 But he answered and said unto him that told him, Who is my mother? and who are my brethren?

12:49 And he stretched forth his hand toward his disciples, and said, Behold my mother and my brethren!

12:50 **For whosoever shall do the will of my Father which is in heaven, the same is my brother, and sister, and mother.**

back forward stop refresh home favorites

http://www.parables1.christ

13:1 The same day went Jesus out of the house, and sat by the sea side.

13:2 And great multitudes were gathered together unto him, so that he went into a ship, and sat; and the whole multitude stood on the shore.

13:3 And he spake many things unto them in **parables**, saying, Behold, a sower went forth to sow;

13:4 And when he sowed, some seeds fell by the way side, and the fowls came and devoured them up:

13:5 Some fell upon stony places, where they had not much earth: and forthwith they sprung up, because they had no deepness of earth:

13:6 And when the sun was up, they were scorched; and because they had no root, they withered away.

13:7 And some fell among thorns;
and the thorns sprung up,
and choked them:

13:8 But other fell into good ground, and brought forth fruit, some an hundredfold, some sixtyfold, some thirtyfold.

13:9 Who hath ears to hear, let him hear.

13:10 And the disciples came, and said unto him, Why speakest thou unto them in **parables**?

13:11 He answered and said unto them, Because it is given unto you **to know the mysteries of the kingdom** of heaven, but to them it is not given.

13:12 For whosoever hath, to him shall be given, and he shall have more abundance: but whosoever hath not, from him shall be taken away even that he hath.

13:13 Therefore speak I to them in **parables**: because they seeing see not; and hearing they hear not, neither do they understand.

13:14 And in them is fulfilled the prophecy of Esaias, which saith, By hearing ye shall hear, and shall not understand; and seeing ye shall see, and shall not perceive:

back forward stop refresh home favorites

http://www.parables2.christ

13:15 For this people's heart is waxed gross, and their ears are
dull of hearing, and their eyes they have closed; lest at any
time they should see with their eyes and hear with their
ears, and should **understand with their heart**, and
should be converted, and I should heal them.

13:16 But blessed are your eyes, for they see: and your ears, for
they hear.

13:17 For verily I say unto you, That many prophets and
righteous men have desired to see those things which ye
see, and have not seen them; and to hear those things
which ye hear, and have not heard them.

13:18 Hear ye therefore the parable of the sower.

13:19 When any one **heareth the word of the kingdom**, and
understandeth it not, then
cometh the wicked one,
and catcheth away that
which was sown in his
heart. This is he which
received seed by the way
side.

mysteries

13:20 But he that received the seed into stony places, the same
is **he that heareth the word, and anon with joy
receiveth it;**

13:21 Yet hath he not root in himself, but dureth for a while:
for when tribulation or persecution ariseth because of the
word, by and by he is offended.

13:22 He also that received seed among the thorns is he that
heareth the word; and the care of this world, and the
deceitfulness of riches, choke the word, and he becometh
unfruitful.

13:23 But he that received seed into the good ground is he that
heareth the word, and understandeth it; which also
beareth fruit, and bringeth forth, some an hundredfold,
some sixty, some thirty.

13:24 Another parable put he forth unto them, saying, The
kingdom of heaven is likened unto a man which sowed
good seed in his field:

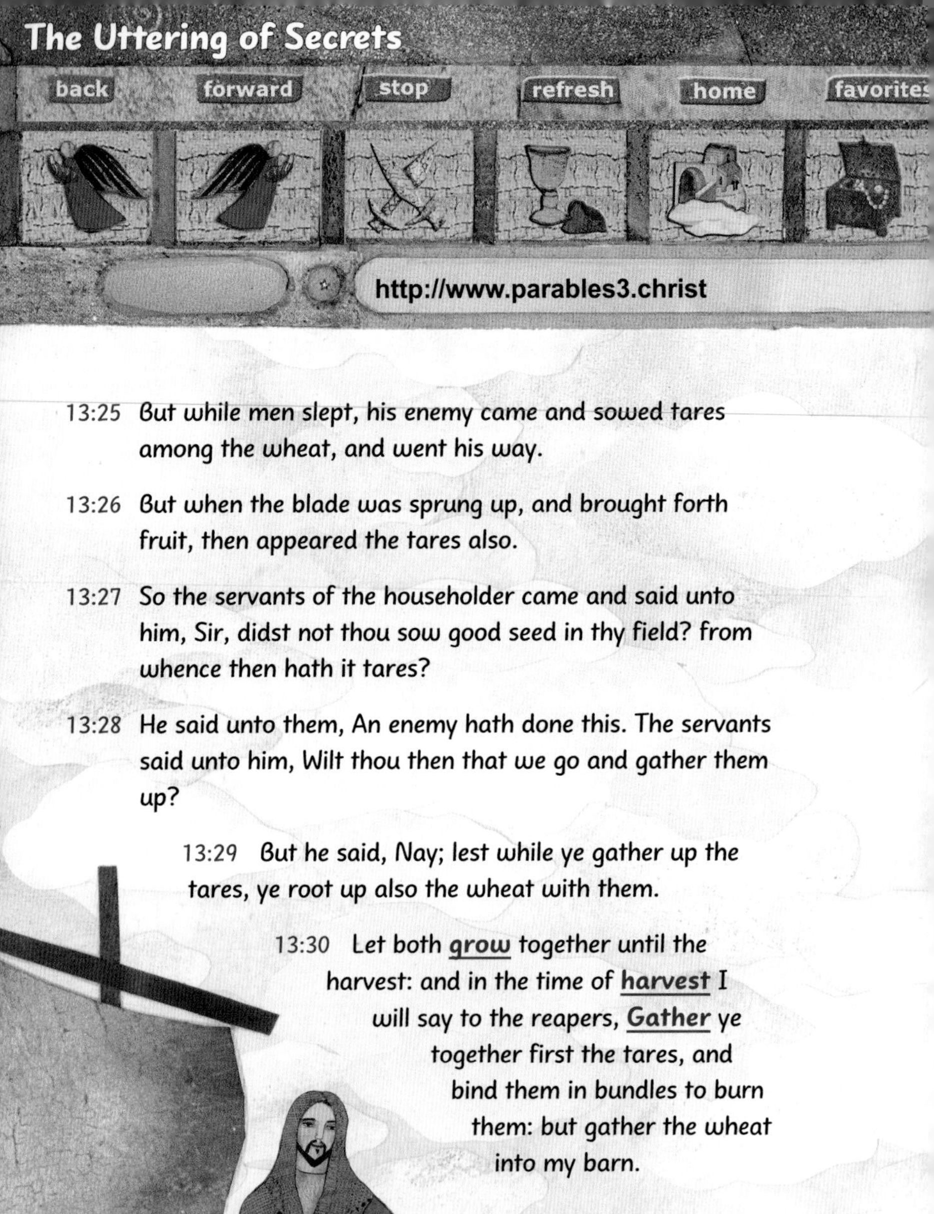

13:25 But while men slept, his enemy came and sowed tares
among the wheat, and went his way.

13:26 But when the blade was sprung up, and brought forth
fruit, then appeared the tares also.

13:27 So the servants of the householder came and said unto
him, Sir, didst not thou sow good seed in thy field? from
whence then hath it tares?

13:28 He said unto them, An enemy hath done this. The servants
said unto him, Wilt thou then that we go and gather them
up?

13:29 But he said, Nay; lest while ye gather up the
tares, ye root up also the wheat with them.

13:30 Let both grow together until the
harvest: and in the time of harvest I
will say to the reapers, Gather ye
together first the tares, and
bind them in bundles to burn
them: but gather the wheat
into my barn.

secrets

13:31 Another **parable** put he forth unto them, saying, The kingdom of heaven is like to a grain of mustard seed, which a man took, and sowed in his field:

13:32 Which indeed is the least of all seeds: but when it is grown, it is the greatest among herbs, and becometh a tree, so that the birds of the air come and lodge in the branches thereof.

13:33 Another **parable** spake he unto them; The kingdom of heaven is like unto leaven, which a woman took, and hid in three measures of meal, till the whole was leavened.

13:34 **All these things spake Jesus unto the multitude in parables; and without a parable spake he not unto them:**

13:35 That it might be fulfilled which was spoken by the prophet, saying, I will open my mouth in **parables**; I will utter things which have been kept **secret** from the foundation of the world.

13:36 Then Jesus sent the multitude away, and went into the house: and his disciples came unto him, saying, Declare unto us the **parable** of the tares of the field.

13:37 He answered and said unto them, He that soweth the good seed is the Son of man;

13:38 The field is the world; the good seed are the **children** of the **kingdom**; but the tares are the children of the wicked one;

13:39 The enemy that sowed them is the devil; the harvest is the end of the world; and the reapers are the angels.

13:40 As therefore the tares are gathered and burned in the fire; so shall it be in the end of this world.

13:41 The Son of man shall send forth his angels, and they shall gather out of his kingdom all things that offend, and them which do iniquity;

13:42 And shall cast them into a furnace of fire: there shall be
wailing and gnashing of teeth.

13:43 Then shall the righteous shine forth as the sun in the
kingdom of their Father. Who hath ears to hear,
let him hear.

13:44 Again, the kingdom of **heaven** is like unto **treasure** hid
in a field; the which when a man hath found, he **hideth**,
and for **joy** thereof goeth and selleth all that he hath, and
buyeth that field.

13:45 Again, the kingdom of heaven is like unto a merchant man,
seeking goodly pearls:

13:46 Who, when he had found one pearl of great price, went
and sold all that he had, and bought it.

Heaven Like A Net

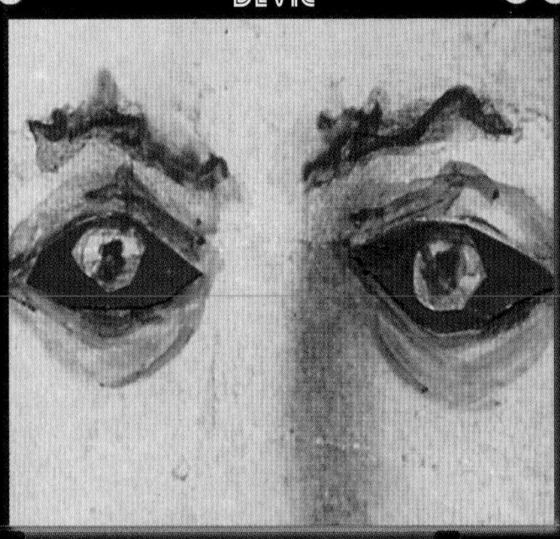

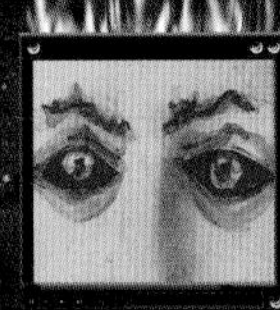

13:47 Again, the kingdom of heaven is like unto a
net, that was cast into the sea, and gathered
of every kind:

13:48 Which, when it was full, they drew to shore,
and sat down, and gathered the good into
vessels, but **CAST THE BAD AWAY**.

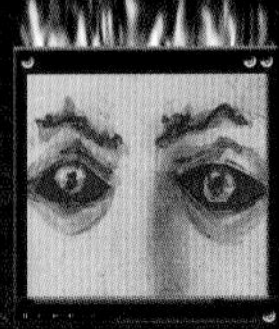

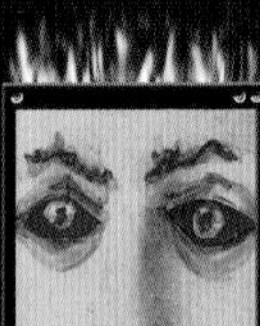

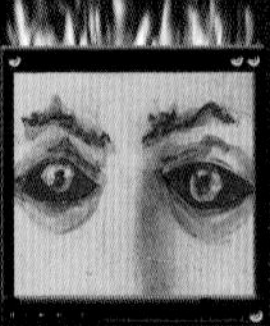

trash

Jesus

Jesus

Jesus

13:49 So shall it be at the end of the world: the
angels shall come forth, and **sever the
wicked from among the just,**

13:50 And shall cast them into the furnace of
fire: there shall be wailing and gnashing
of teeth.

Jesus

Matthew 13:47

The kingdom of heaven is like a net.

Jesus

Jesus

13:51 Jesus saith unto them, Have ye understood all these things? They say unto him, Yea, Lord.

13:52 Then said he unto them, Therefore every scribe which is instructed unto the kingdom of heaven is like unto a man that is an householder, which bringeth forth out of his treasure things new and old.

13:53 And it came to pass, that when Jesus had finished these parables, he departed thence.

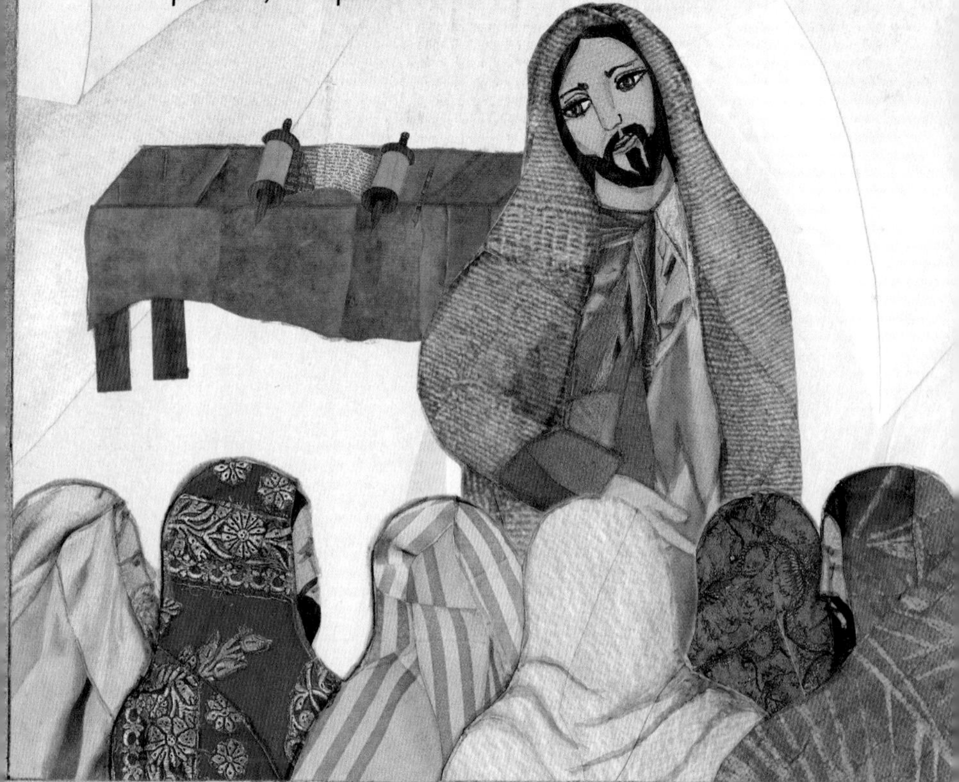

travel
mail
print
chat
A PROPHET IS NOT WITHOUT HONOUR, SAVE IN HIS OWN COUNTRY, AND IN HIS OWN HOUSE.

13:54 And when he was come into his own country, he taught them in their synagogue, insomuch that they were astonished, and said, Whence hath this man this wisdom, and these mighty works?

13:55 Is not this the carpenter's son? is not his mother called Mary? and his brethren, James, and Joses, and Simon, and Judas?

13:56 And his sisters, are they not all with us? Whence then hath this man all these things?

13:57 And they were offended in him. But Jesus said unto them, A prophet is not without honour, save in his own country, and in his own house.

13:58 And he did not many mighty works there because of their **UNBELIEF**.

Beheading of John the Baptist

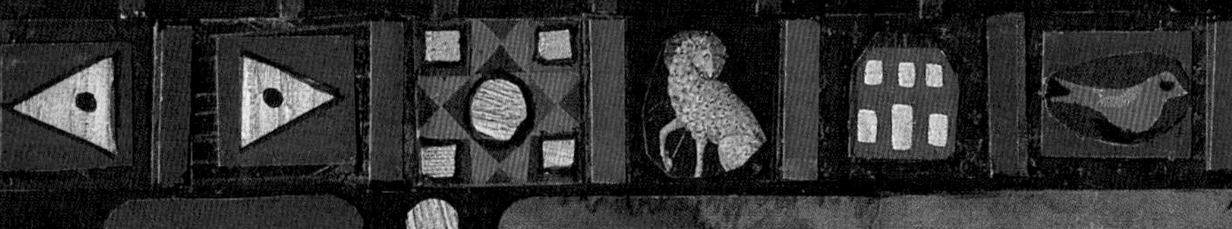

14:1 At that time Herod the tetrarch heard of the fame of
Jesus,

14:2 And said unto his servants, This is John the Baptist; he is
risen from the dead; and therefore mighty works do shew
forth themselves in him.

14:3 For Herod had laid hold on John, and bound him, and put
him in prison for Herodias' sake, his brother Philip's wife.

14:4 For John said unto him, It is not lawful for thee to have
her.

14:5 And when he would have put him to DEATH, he feared
the multitude, because they counted him as a prophet.

14:6 But when Herod's birthday was kept, the daughter of
Herodias danced before them, and pleased Herod.

14:7 Whereupon he promised with an oath to give her
whatsoever she would ask.

14:8 And she, being before instructed of her mother, said, Give
me here John Baptist's head in a charger.

14:9 And the king was SORRY: nevertheless for the oath's sake,
and them which sat with him at meat, he commanded it
to be given her.

14:10 And he sent, and BEHEADED JOHN in the prison.

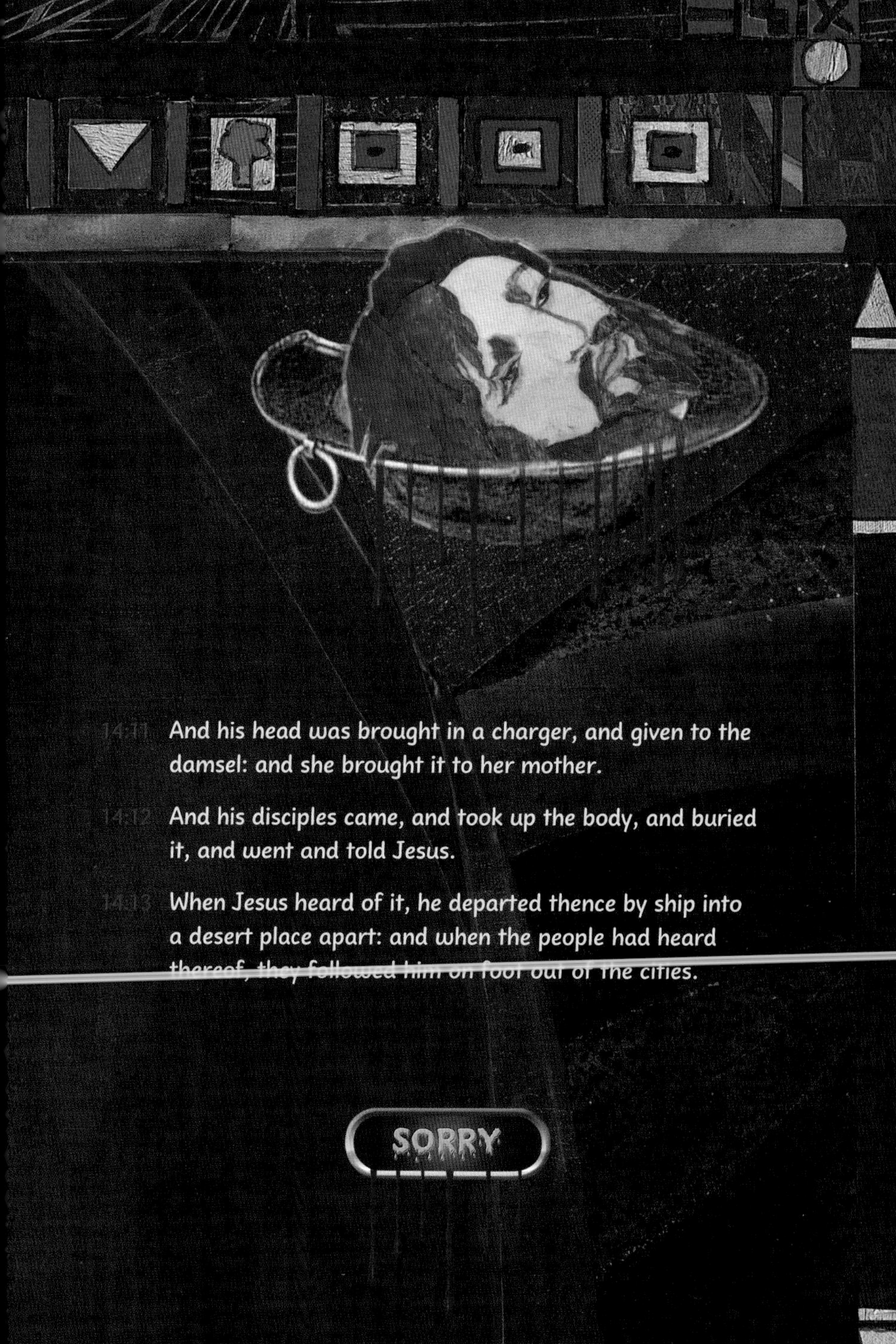

14:11 And his head was brought in a charger, and given to the
damsel: and she brought it to her mother.

14:12 And his disciples came, and took up the body, and buried
it, and went and told Jesus.

14:13 When Jesus heard of it, he departed thence by ship into
a desert place apart: and when the people had heard
thereof, they followed him on foot out of the cities.

Feeding the Hungry 1

14:14 And Jesus went forth, and saw a great multitude, and
was moved with compassion toward them, and he healed
their sick.

14:15 And when it was evening, his disciples came to him,
saying, This is a desert place, and the time is now past;
send the multitude away, that they may go into the
villages, and buy themselves victuals.

14:16 But Jesus said unto them, They need not depart; give ye
them to eat.

14:17 And they say unto him, We have here but five loaves, and
two fishes.

14:18 He said, Bring them hither to me.

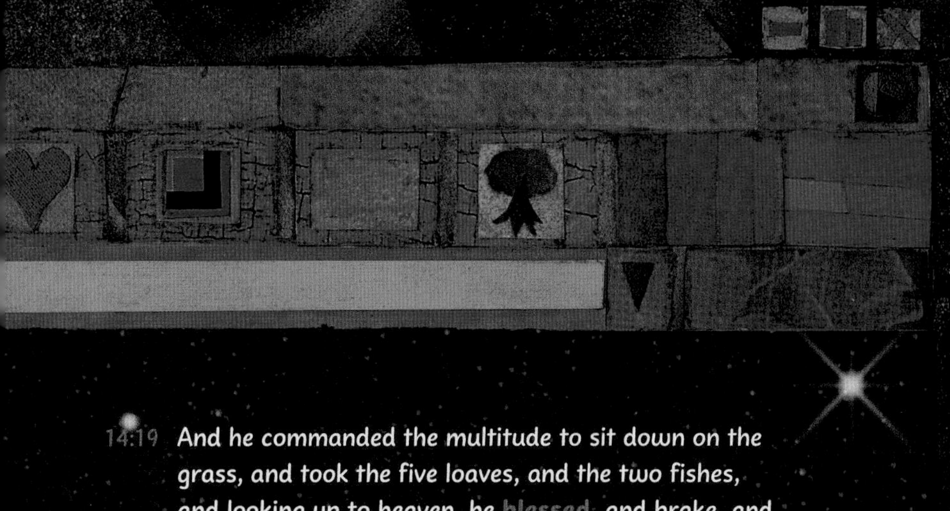

14:19 And he commanded the multitude to sit down on the
grass, and took the five loaves, and the two fishes,
and looking up to heaven, he blessed, and brake, and
gave the loaves to his disciples, and the disciples to the
multitude.

14:20 And they did all eat, and were filled: and they took up of
the fragments that remained twelve baskets full.

14:21 And they that had eaten were about five thousand men,
beside women and children.

14:22 And straightway Jesus constrained his disciples to get
into a ship, and to go before him unto the other side,
while he sent the multitudes away.

compassion

14:23 And when he had sent the multitudes away, he went up into a mountain apart to pray: and when the evening was come, he was there alone.

14:24 But the ship was now in the midst of the sea, tossed with waves: for the wind was contrary.

14:25 And in the fourth watch of the night Jesus went unto them, walking on the sea.

14:26 And when the disciples saw him walking on the sea, they were troubled, saying, It is a spirit; and they cried out for fear.

14:27 But straightway Jesus spake unto them, saying, Be of good cheer; it is I; be not afraid.

14:28 And Peter answered him and said, Lord, if it be thou, bid me come unto thee on the water.

faith

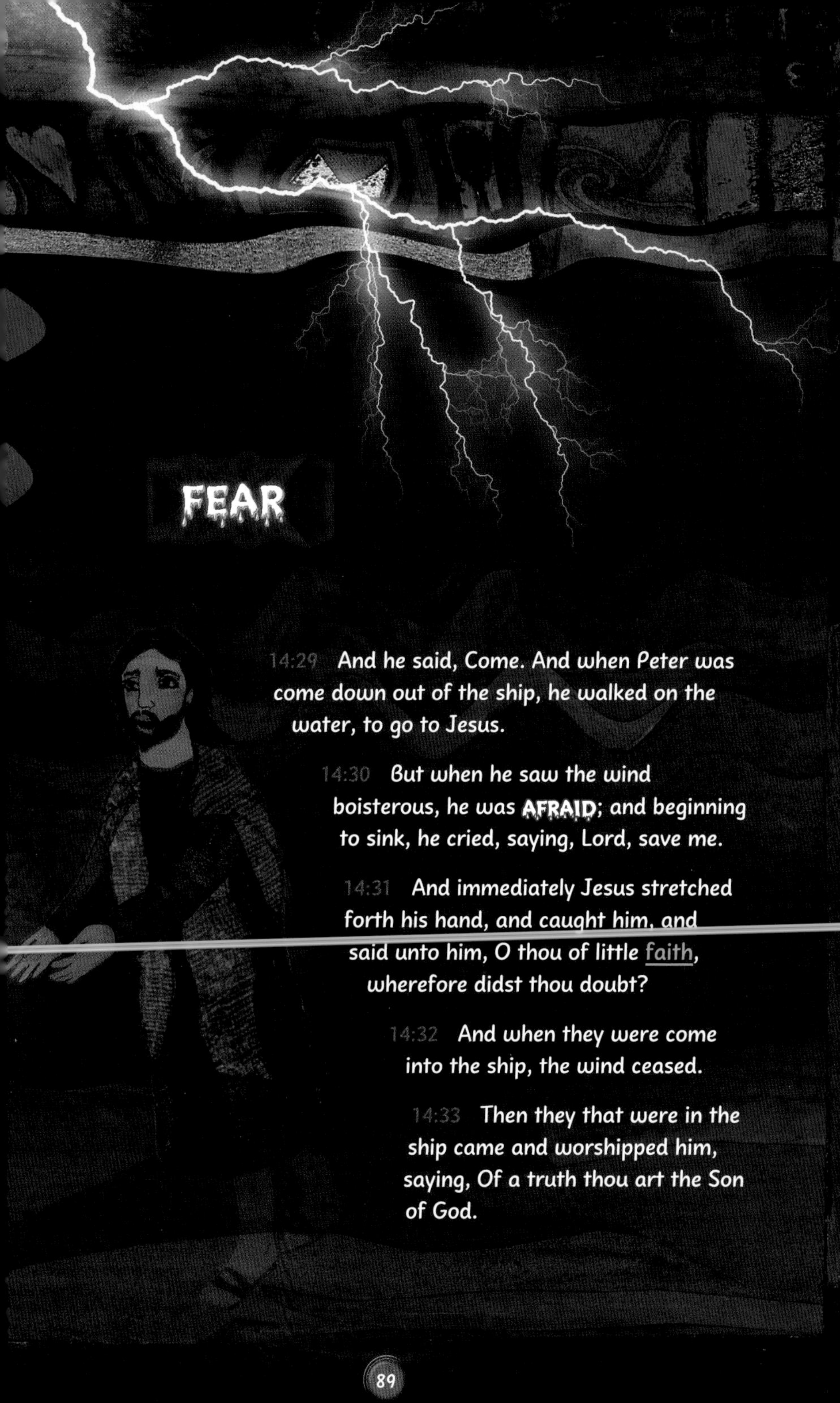

FEAR

14:29 And he said, Come. And when Peter was
come down out of the ship, he walked on the
water, to go to Jesus.

14:30 But when he saw the wind
boisterous, he was **AFRAID**; and beginning
to sink, he cried, saying, Lord, save me.

14:31 And immediately Jesus stretched
forth his hand, and caught him, and
said unto him, O thou of little faith,
wherefore didst thou doubt?

14:32 And when they were come
into the ship, the wind ceased.

14:33 Then they that were in the
ship came and worshipped him,
saying, Of a truth thou art the Son
of God.

BLIND

14:34 And when they were gone over, they came into
the land of Gennesaret.

14:35 And when the men of that place had
knowledge of him, they sent out into all that country
round about, and brought unto him all that were
diseased;

14:36 And besought him that they might only touch
the hem of his garment: and as many as touched were
made perfectly whole.

15:1 Then came to Jesus scribes and Pharisees, which were of Jerusalem, saying,

15:2 Why do thy disciples **TRANSGRESS THE TRADITION** of the elders? for they wash not their hands when they eat bread.

15:3 But he answered and said unto them, Why do ye also transgress the commandment of God by your tradition?

15:4 For God commanded, saying, Honour thy father and mother: and, He that curseth father or mother, let him die the death.

15:5 But ye say, Whosoever shall say to his father or his mother, It is a gift, by whatsoever thou mightest be profited by me;

15:6 And honour not his father or his mother, he shall be free. Thus have ye made the commandment of God of none effect by your **TRADITION**.

15:7 Ye hypocrites, well did Esaias prophesy of you, saying,

15:8 This people draweth nigh unto me with their mouth, and honoureth me with their **LIPS**; but their **HEART IS FAR** from me.

15:9 But in **VAIN** they do worship me, teaching for doctrines the **COMMANDMENTS OF MEN**.

15:10 And he called the multitude, and said unto them, Hear, and understand:

15:11 Not that which goeth into the mouth defileth a man; but that which cometh out of the mouth, this defileth a man.

15:12 Then came his disciples, and said unto him, Knowest thou that the Pharisees were offended, after they heard this saying?

15:13 But he answered and said, Every plant, which my heavenly Father hath not planted, shall be rooted up.

15:14 Let them alone: they be **BLIND LEADERS OF THE BLIND**. And if the blind lead the blind, both shall fall into the ditch.

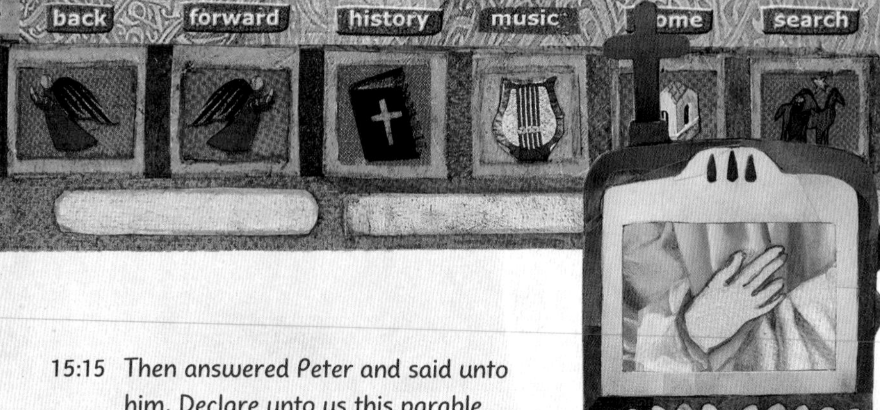

15:15 Then answered Peter and said unto him, Declare unto us this parable.

15:16 And Jesus said, Are ye also yet without understanding?

15:17 Do not ye yet understand, that whatsoever entereth in at the mouth goeth into the belly, and is cast out into the draught?

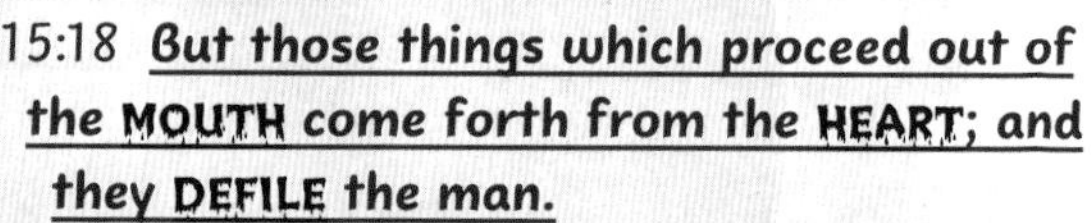

15:18 **But those things which proceed out of the MOUTH come forth from the HEART; and they DEFILE the man.**

15:19 For out of the heart proceed evil thoughts, murders, adulteries, fornications, thefts, false witness, blasphemies:

15:20 These are the things which defile a man: but to eat with unwashen hands defileth not a man.

15:21 Then Jesus went thence, and departed into the coasts of Tyre and Sidon.

Matthew 15:18

Things which proceed out of the mouth come forth from the heart.

15:22 And, behold, a woman of Canaan came out of the same coasts, and cried unto him, saying, Have mercy on me, O Lord, thou son of David; my daughter is grievously vexed with a **DEVIL.**

15:23 But he answered her not a word. And his disciples came and besought him, saying, Send her away; for she crieth after us.

15:24 But he answered and said, I am not sent but unto the lost sheep of the house of Israel.

15:25 Then came she and worshipped him, saying, Lord, help me.

15:26 But he answered and said, It is not meet to take the children's bread, and to cast it to dogs.

15:27 And she said, Truth, Lord: yet the dogs eat of the crumbs which fall from their masters' table.

15:28 Then Jesus answered and said unto her, **O woman, great is thy faith: be it unto thee even as thou wilt.** And her daughter was made whole from that very hour.

back forward stop refresh home favorite

http://www.feedingthehungry.christ

15:29 And Jesus departed from thence, and came nigh unto the sea of Galilee; and went up into a mountain, and sat down there.

15:30 And great multitudes came unto him, having with them those that were lame, blind, dumb, maimed, and many others, and cast them down at Jesus' feet; and he healed them:

15:31 Insomuch that the multitude wondered, when they saw the dumb to speak, the maimed to be whole, the lame to walk, and the blind to see: and they glorified the God of Israel.

15:32 Then Jesus called his disciples unto him, and said, I have **compassion on the multitude**, because they continue with me now three days, and have nothing to eat: and I will not send them away fasting, lest they faint in the way.

15:33 And his disciples say unto him, Whence should we have so much bread in the wilderness, as to fill so great a multitude?

search history mail print

15:34 And Jesus saith unto them, How many loaves have ye?
And they said, Seven, and a few little fishes.

15:35 And he commanded the multitude to sit down on the
ground.

15:36 And he took the seven loaves and the fishes, and **gave
thanks**, and brake them, and gave to his disciples, and the
disciples to the multitude.

15:37 **And they did all eat, and were filled**: and they took up
of the broken meat that was left seven baskets full.

15:38 And they that did eat were four thousand men, beside
women and children.

15:39 And he sent away the multitude, and took ship, and came
into the coasts of Magdala.

thanks

16:1 The Pharisees also with the Sadducees came, and
tempting desired him that he would shew them a
sign from heaven.

16:2 He answered and said unto them, When it is evening, ye
say, It will be fair weather: for the sky is red.

16:3 And in the morning, It will be foul weather to day: for the
sky is red and lowering. O ye hypocrites, ye can discern
the face of the sky; but can ye not discern the
signs of the times?

A wicked and adulterous generation seeketh after a sign;
and there shall no sign be given unto it, but the sign of
the prophet Jonas. And he left them, and departed.

And when his disciples were come to the other side,
they had forgotten to take bread.

Then Jesus said unto them, Take heed and
beware of the leaven of the Pharisees and
of the Sadducees.

16:7 And they reasoned among themselves, saying, It is
because we have taken no bread.

16:8 Which when Jesus perceived, he said unto them, O ye of
little faith, why reason ye among yourselves, because ye
have brought no bread?

16:9 Do ye not yet understand, neither remember the five
loaves of the five thousand, and how many baskets ye
took up?

16:10 Neither the seven loaves of the four thousand, and how
many baskets ye took up?

16:11 How is it that ye do not understand that I spake it not
to you concerning bread, that ye should beware of the
leaven of the Pharisees and of the Sadducees?

16:12 Then understood they how that he bade them not
beware of the leaven of bread, but of the doctrine of the
Pharisees and of the Sadducees.

signs times

16:13 When Jesus came into the coasts of Caesarea Philippi, he asked his disciples, saying, Whom do men say that I the Son of man am?

16:14 And they said, Some say that thou art John the Baptist: some, Elias; and others, Jeremias, or one of the prophets.

16:15 He saith unto them, But whom say ye that I am?

16:16 And Simon Peter answered and said, **Thou art the Christ, the Son of the living God.**

16:17 And Jesus answered and said unto him, Blessed art thou, Simon Barjona: for flesh and blood hath not revealed it unto thee, but my Father which is in heaven.

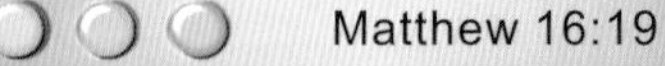

I will give unto thee the keys of the kingdom of heaven.

16:18 And I say also unto thee, That thou art
Peter, and **upon this rock I will build
my church**; and the gates of hell shall
not prevail against it.

16:19 And **I will give unto thee the keys
of the kingdom of heaven**: and
whatsoever thou shalt bind on
earth shall be bound in heaven: and
whatsoever thou shalt loose on earth
shall be loosed in heaven.

16:20 Then charged he his disciples that
they should tell no man that he was
Jesus the Christ.

16:21 From that time forth began Jesus to
shew unto his disciples, how that he
must go unto Jerusalem, and suffer
many things of the elders and chief
priests and scribes, and be killed, and
be raised again the third day.

16:22 Then Peter took him, and began to
rebuke him, saying, Be it far from
thee, Lord: this shall not be unto thee.

16:23 But he turned, and said unto Peter,
Get thee behind me, Satan: thou
art an offence unto me: for thou
savourest not the things that be of
God, but those that be of men.

16:24 Then said Jesus unto his disciples, If
any man will come after me, let him
deny himself, and take up his cross,
and follow me.

16:25 For whosoever will **save** his life shall
lose it: and whosoever will lose his
life for my sake shall find it.

16:26 For what is a man profited, if he
shall gain the whole world, and lose
his own soul? or what shall a man
give in exchange for his soul?

16:27 For the Son of man shall come in the
glory of his Father with his angels;
and then he shall **reward** every man
according to his works.

16:28 Verily I say unto you, There be some
standing here, which shall not taste
of death, till they see the Son of man
coming in his **kingdom**.

17:1 And after six days Jesus taketh
Peter, James, and John his brother,
and bringeth them up into an high
mountain apart,

17:2 And was **transfigured** before them:
and his face did shine as the sun, and
his raiment was white as the light.

17:3 And, behold, there appeared unto them Moses and Elias talking with him.

17:4 Then answered Peter, and said unto Jesus, Lord, it is good for us to be here: if thou wilt, let us make here three tabernacles; one for thee, and one for Moses, and one for Elias.

17:5 While he yet spake, behold, a bright cloud overshadowed them: and behold a voice out of the cloud, which said, This is my beloved Son, in whom I am well pleased; hear ye him.

17:6 And when the disciples heard it, they fell on their face, and were sore afraid.

17:7 And Jesus came and touched them, and said, **Arise, and be not afraid.**

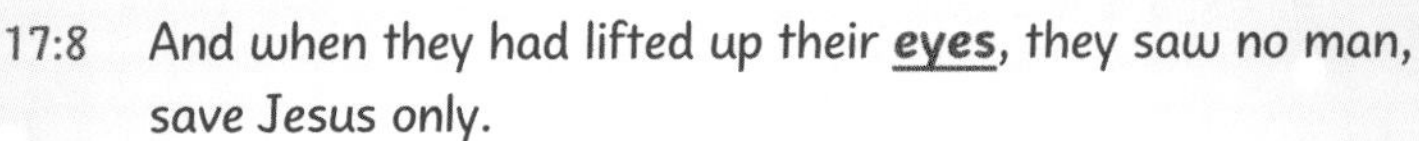

17:8 And when they had lifted up their **eyes**, they saw no man, save Jesus only.

17:9 And as they came down from the mountain, Jesus charged them, saying, Tell the **vision** to no man, until the Son of man be risen again from the dead.

17:10 And his disciples asked him, saying, Why then say the scribes that Elias must first come?

17:11 And Jesus answered and said unto them, Elias truly shall first come, and **restore** all things.

17:12 But I say unto you, That Elias is come already, and they knew him not, but have done unto him whatsoever they listed. Likewise shall also the Son of man suffer of them.

17:13 Then the disciples understood that he spake unto them of John the Baptist.

17:14 And when they were come to the multitude, there came to him a certain man, kneeling down to him, and saying,

17:15 **Lord, have mercy** on my son: for he is lunatick, and sore vexed: for ofttimes he falleth into the fire, and oft into the water.

17:16 And I brought him to thy disciples, and they could not cure him.

17:17 Then Jesus answered and said, O faithless and perverse generation, how long shall I be with you? how long shall I suffer you? bring him hither to me.

17:18 And Jesus rebuked the devil; and he departed out of him: and the child was cured from that very hour.

17:19 Then came the disciples to Jesus apart, and said, Why could not we cast him out?

17:20 And Jesus said unto them, Because of your unbelief:
for verily I say unto you,

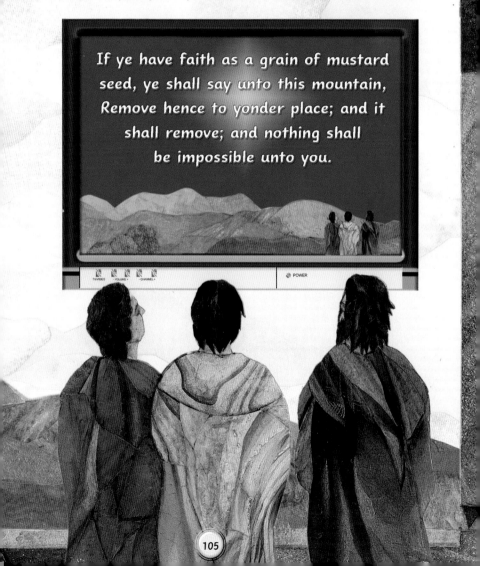

If ye have faith as a grain of mustard seed, ye shall say unto this mountain, Remove hence to yonder place; and it shall remove; and nothing shall be impossible unto you.

Matthew 18:3

Except ye be converted, and become as little children, ye shall not enter into the kingdom of heaven.

17:22 And while they abode in Galilee, Jesus said unto them, The Son of man shall be betrayed into the hands of men:

17:23 And they shall kill him, and the third day he shall be raised again. And they were exceeding sorry.

17:24 And when they were come to Capernaum, they that received tribute money came to Peter, and said, Doth not your master pay tribute?

17:25 He saith, Yes. And when he was come into the house, Jesus prevented him, saying, What thinkest thou, Simon? of whom do the kings of the earth take custom or tribute? of their own children, or of strangers?

17:26 Peter saith unto him, Of strangers. Jesus saith unto him, Then are the **children free**.

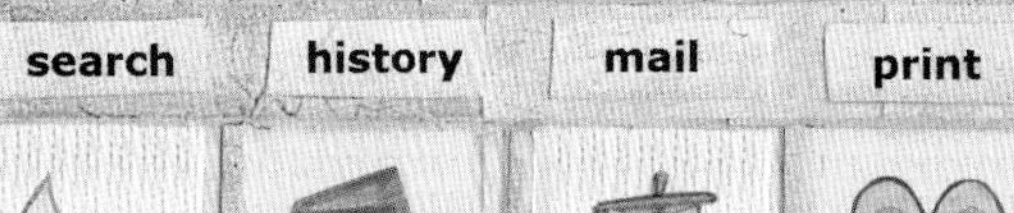

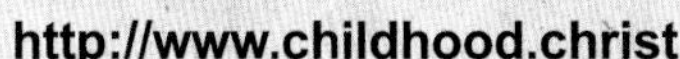

17:27 Notwithstanding, lest we should offend them, go thou to the sea, and cast an hook, and take up the fish that first cometh up; and when thou hast opened his mouth, thou shalt find a piece of money: that take, and give unto them for me and thee.

18:1 At the same time came the disciples unto Jesus, saying, Who is the **greatest** in the kingdom of **heaven**?

18:2 And Jesus called a little **child** unto him, and set him in the midst of them,

18:3 And said, Verily I say unto you, Except ye be converted, and **become as little children**, ye shall not enter into the kingdom of heaven.

18:4 Whosoever therefore shall **humble** himself as this little **child**, the same is greatest in the kingdom of **heaven**.

18:5 And whoso shall receive one such little child in my name receiveth me.

(children only)

back forward stop refresh home search favorite

Matthew 18:14

It is not the will of your Father which is in heaven, that one of these little ones should perish.

18:6 But whoso shall offend one of these little ones which believe in me, it were better for him that a millstone were hanged about his neck, and that he were drowned in the depth of the sea.

18:7 Woe unto the world because of offences! for it must needs be that offences come; but woe to that man by whom the offence cometh!

18:8 Wherefore if thy hand or thy foot offend thee, cut them off, and cast them from thee: it is better for thee to enter into life halt or maimed, rather than having two hands or two feet to be cast into everlasting fire.

18:9 And if thine eye offend thee, pluck it out, and cast it from thee: it is better for thee to enter into life with one eye, rather than having two eyes to be cast into hell fire.

18:10 Take heed that ye despise not one of these little ones; for I say unto you, That in heaven their angels do always behold the face of my Father which is in heaven.

18:11 For the Son of man is come to **Save** that
which was lost.

18:12 How think ye? if a man have an hundred sheep, and one of
them be gone astray, doth he not leave the ninety and
nine, and goeth into the mountains, and seeketh that
which is gone astray?

18:13 And if so be that he find it, verily I say unto
you, he rejoiceth more of that sheep, than of the
ninety and nine which went not astray.

18:14 Even so it is not the will of your
Father which is in heaven, that one of
these little ones should perish.

18:15 Moreover if thy brother shall trespass against thee, go and tell him his fault between thee and him alone: if he shall hear thee, thou hast gained thy brother.

18:16 But if he will not hear thee, then take with thee one or two more, that in the mouth of two or three witnesses every word may be established.

18:17 And if he shall neglect to hear them, tell it unto the church: but if he neglect to hear the church, let him be unto thee as an heathen man and a publican.

18:18 Verily I say unto you, **Whatsoever ye shall bind on earth shall be bound in heaven**: and whatsoever ye shall loose on earth shall be loosed in heaven.

18:19 Again I say unto you, That if two of you shall agree on earth as touching any thing that they shall ask, it shall be done for them of my Father which is in heaven.

18:20 For **where two or three are gathered together in my name, there am I in the midst of them.**

18:21 Then came Peter to him, and said, Lord, how oft shall my brother sin against me, and I forgive him? till seven times?

18:22 Jesus saith unto him, I say not unto thee, Until seven times: but, Until seventy times seven.

Where two or three are gathered together in my name, there am I in the midst of them.

18:23 Therefore is the kingdom of heaven likened unto a certain king, which would take account of his servants.

18:24 And when he had begun to reckon, one was brought unto him, which owed him ten thousand talents.

18:25 But forasmuch as he had not to pay, his lord commanded him to be sold, and his wife, and children, and all that he had, and payment to be made.

18:26 The servant therefore fell down, and worshipped him, saying, Lord, have **patience** with me, and I will pay thee all.

18:27 Then the lord of that servant was moved with **compassion**, and loosed him, and **forgave** him the debt.

18:28 But the same servant went out, and found one of his fellowservants, which owed him an hundred pence: and he laid hands on him, and took him by the throat, saying, Pay me that thou owest.

18:29 And his fellowservant fell down at his feet, and besought him, saying, Have **patience** with me, and I will pay thee all.

18:30 And he would not: but went and cast him into prison, till he should pay the debt.

18:31 So when his fellowservants saw what was done, they were very sorry, and came and told unto their lord all that was done.

18:32 Then his lord, after that he had called him, said unto him, O thou wicked servant, I **forgave** thee all that debt, because thou desiredst me:

18:33 Shouldest not thou also have had **compassion** on thy fellowservant, even as I had pity on thee?

18:34 And his lord was wroth, and delivered him to the tormentors, till he should pay all that was due unto him.

18:35 So likewise shall my heavenly Father do also unto you, if ye **from your hearts forgive** not every one his brother their trespasses.

Matthew 19:6

What God hath joined together, let not man put asunder.

19:1 And it came to pass, that when Jesus
had finished these sayings, he departed from
Galilee, and came into the coasts of Judaea
beyond Jordan;

19:2 And great multitudes followed him; and he healed them
there.

19:3 The Pharisees also came unto him, tempting him, and
saying unto him, Is it lawful for a man to put away his
wife for every cause?

19:4 And he answered and said unto them, Have ye not read,
that he which made them at the beginning made them
male and female,

19:5 And said, For this cause shall a **man** leave father and
mother, and shall cleave to his **wife**: and they twain shall
be **one flesh**?

19:6 Wherefore they are no more twain, but one flesh. What
therefore God hath joined together, let not man put
asunder.

19:7 They say unto him, Why did Moses then command to give a writing of divorcement, and to put her away?

19:8 He saith unto them, Moses because of the hardness of your hearts suffered you to put away your wives: but from the beginning it was not so.

19:9 And I say unto you, Whosoever shall put away his wife, except it be for fornication, and shall marry another, committeth adultery: and whoso marrieth her which is put away doth commit adultery.

19:10 His disciples say unto him, If the case of the man be so with his wife, it is not good to marry.

19:11 But he said unto them, All men cannot receive this saying, save they to whom it is given.

19:12 For there are some eunuchs, which were so born from their mother's womb: and there are some eunuchs, which were made eunuchs of men: and there be eunuchs, which have made themselves eunuchs for the kingdom of heaven's sake. He that is able to receive it, let him receive it.

19:13 Then were there brought unto him little children, that he should put his hands on them, and pray: and the disciples rebuked them.

children heaven

19:14 But Jesus said, Suffer **little children**, and forbid them not,
to come unto me: for of such is the **kingdom of heaven**.

19:15 And he laid his hands on them, and departed thence.

19:16 And, behold, one came and said unto him, Good Master,
what good thing shall I do, that I may have eternal life?

19:17 And he said unto him, Why callest thou me good? there is
none good but one, that is, God: but if thou wilt enter into
life, keep the commandments.

19:18 He saith unto him, Which? Jesus said, Thou shalt do no
murder, Thou shalt not commit adultery, Thou shalt not
steal, Thou shalt not bear false witness,

19:19 Honour thy father and thy mother: and, Thou shalt **love**
thy neighbour as thyself.

19:20 The young man saith unto him, All these things have I kept
from my youth up: what lack I yet?

19:21 Jesus said unto him, If thou wilt be perfect, go and sell
that thou hast, and give to the poor, and thou shalt have
treasure in heaven: and come and follow me.

19:22 But when the young man heard that saying, he went away
sorrowful: for he had great possessions.

19:23 Then said Jesus unto his disciples, Verily I say unto you,
That a rich man shall hardly enter into the kingdom of
heaven.

19:24 And again I say unto you, It is easier for a camel to go
through the eye of a needle, than for a rich man to
enter into the kingdom of God.

19:25 When his disciples heard it, they were exceedingly
amazed, saying, Who then can be saved?

19:26 But Jesus beheld them, and said unto them,
With men this is impossible; but with God all
things are possible.

19:27 Then answered Peter and said unto him,
Behold, we have forsaken all, and followed
thee; what shall we have therefore?

God

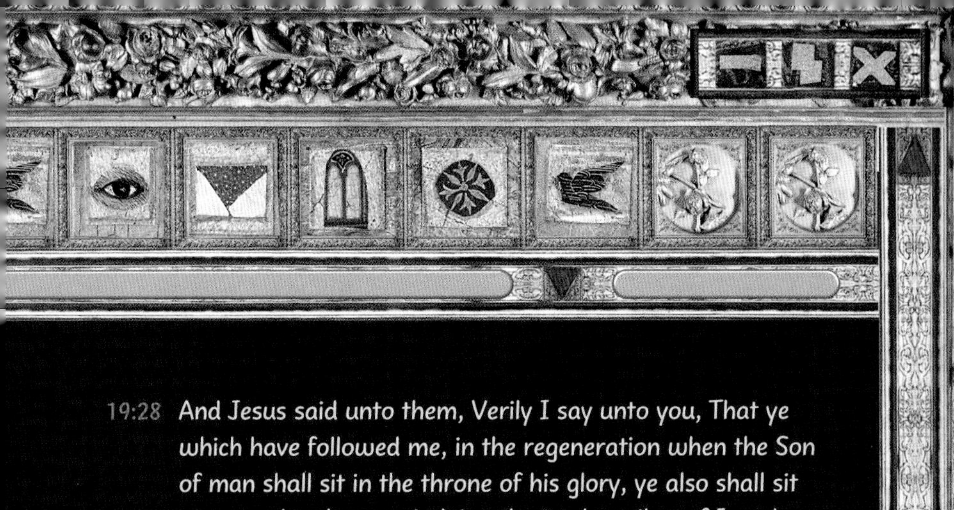

19:28 And Jesus said unto them, Verily I say unto you, That ye
which have followed me, in the regeneration when the Son
of man shall sit in the throne of his glory, ye also shall sit
upon twelve thrones, judging the twelve tribes of Israel.

19:29 And every one that hath forsaken houses, or brethren, or
sisters, or father, or mother, or wife, or children, or lands,
for my name's sake, shall receive an hundredfold, and shall
inherit everlasting life.

19:30 But many that are first shall be last; and the last
shall be first.

20:1 For the kingdom of heaven is like unto a
man that is an householder, which went out
early in the morning to hire labourers into his
vineyard.

20:2 And when he had agreed with the
labourers for a penny a day, he sent them into his
vineyard.

20:3 And he went out about the third hour, and
saw others standing idle in the marketplace,

20:4 And said unto them; Go ye also into the
vineyard, and whatsoever is right I will give you.
And they went their way.

possible

grace

20:5 Again he went out about the sixth
and ninth hour, and did likewise.

20:6 And about **the eleventh hour** he went
out, and found others standing idle, and
saith unto them, Why stand ye here all the
day idle?

20:7 They say unto him, Because no man hath hired
us. He saith unto them, Go ye also into the vineyard;
and whatsoever is right, that shall ye receive.

20:8 So when even was come, the lord of the vineyard saith
unto his steward, Call the labourers, and give them their
hire, beginning from the last unto the first.

20:9 And when they came that were hired about **the eleventh
hour**, they received every man a penny.

20:10 But when the first came, they supposed that they should
have received more; and they likewise received every man
a penny.

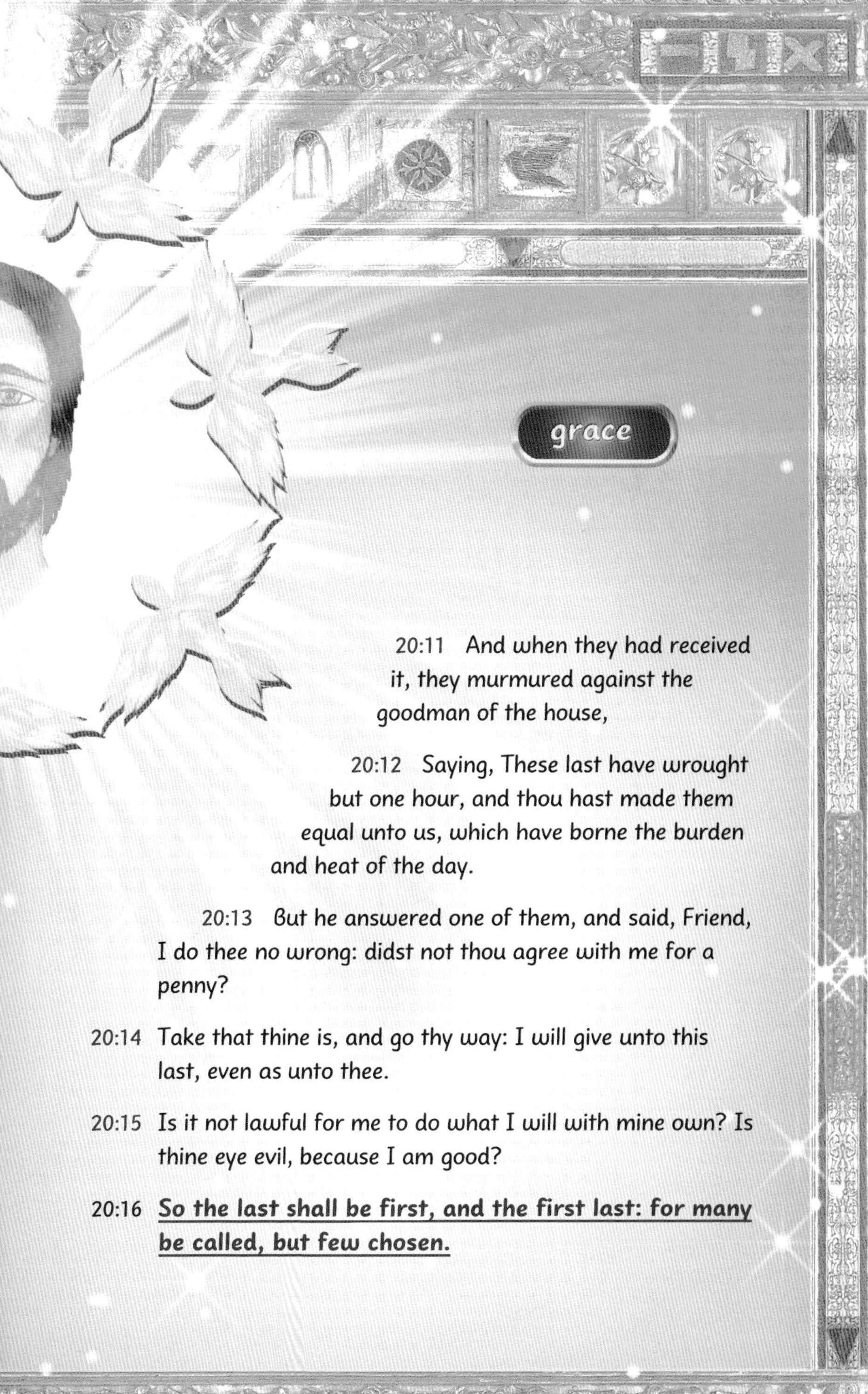

20:11 And when they had received
it, they murmured against the
goodman of the house,

20:12 Saying, These last have wrought
but one hour, and thou hast made them
equal unto us, which have borne the burden
and heat of the day.

20:13 But he answered one of them, and said, Friend,
I do thee no wrong: didst not thou agree with me for a
penny?

20:14 Take that thine is, and go thy way: I will give unto this last, even as unto thee.

20:15 Is it not lawful for me to do what I will with mine own? Is thine eye evil, because I am good?

20:16 **So the last shall be first, and the first last: for many be called, but few chosen.**

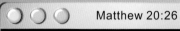

http://www.ministersandserv... ist

Matthew 20:26

Whosoever will be great among you, let him be your minister.

20:17 As Jesus was going up to Jerusalem, he took the twelve disciples aside, and on the way he said to them.

20:18 Behold, we go up to Jerusalem; and the Son of man shall be betrayed unto the chief priests and unto the scribes, and they shall condemn him to death,

20:19 And shall deliver him to the Gentiles to mock, and to scourge, and to crucify him: and the third day he shall rise again.

20:20 Then came to him the mother of Zebedees children with her sons, **worshipping** him, and desiring a certain thing of him.

20:21 And he said unto her, What wilt thou? She saith unto him, Grant that these my two sons may sit, the one on thy right hand, and the other on the left, in thy kingdom.

20:22 But Jesus answered and said, Ye know not what ye ask. Are ye able to drink of the cup that I shall drink of, and to be baptized with the baptism that I am baptized with? They say unto him, We are able.

genuine leaders

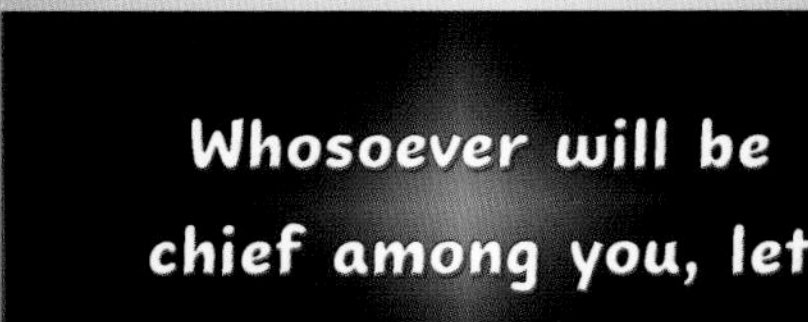
Matthew 20:27
Whosoever will be chief among you, let him be your servant.

20:23 And he saith unto them, Ye shall drink indeed of my cup,
and be baptized with the baptism that I am baptized with:
but to sit on my right hand, and on my left, is not mine to
give, but it shall be given to them for whom it is prepared
of my Father.

20:24 And when the ten heard it, they were moved with
indignation against the two brethren.

20:25 But Jesus called them unto him, and said, Ye know that
the princes of the Gentiles exercise dominion over them,
and they that are great exercise authority upon them.

20:26 But it shall not be so among you: but whosoever will be
great among you, let him be your **minister**;

20:27 And whosoever will be **chief among you**, let him be your
servant:

20:28 Even as the Son of man came not to be ministered unto,
but to minister, and to give his life a ransom for many.

20:29 And as they departed from Jericho, a great multitude followed him.

20:30 And, behold, two blind men sitting by the way side, when they heard that Jesus passed by, cried out, saying, Have mercy on us, O Lord, thou son of David.

20:31 And the multitude rebuked them, because they should hold their peace: but they cried the more, saying, Have mercy on us, O Lord, thou son of David.

20:32 And Jesus stood still, and called them, and said, What will ye that I shall do unto you?

20:33 They say unto him, Lord, that our **eyes** may be **opened.**

20:34 So Jesus had compassion on them, and touched their eyes: and immediately their eyes received sight, and they followed him.

21:1 And when they drew nigh unto Jerusalem, and were come to Bethphage, unto the mount of Olives, then sent Jesus two disciples,

21:2 Saying unto them, Go into the village over against you, and straightway ye shall find an ass tied, and a colt with her: loose them, and bring them unto me.

21:3 And if any man say ought unto you, ye shall say, The Lord hath need of them; and straightway he will send them.

21:4 All this was done, that it might be fulfilled which was spoken by the prophet, saying,

21:5 Tell ye the daughter of Sion, Behold, thy King cometh unto thee, meek, and sitting upon an ass, and a colt the foal of an ass.

21:6 And the disciples went, and did as Jesus commanded them,

21:7 And brought the ass, and the colt, and put on them their clothes, and they set him thereon.

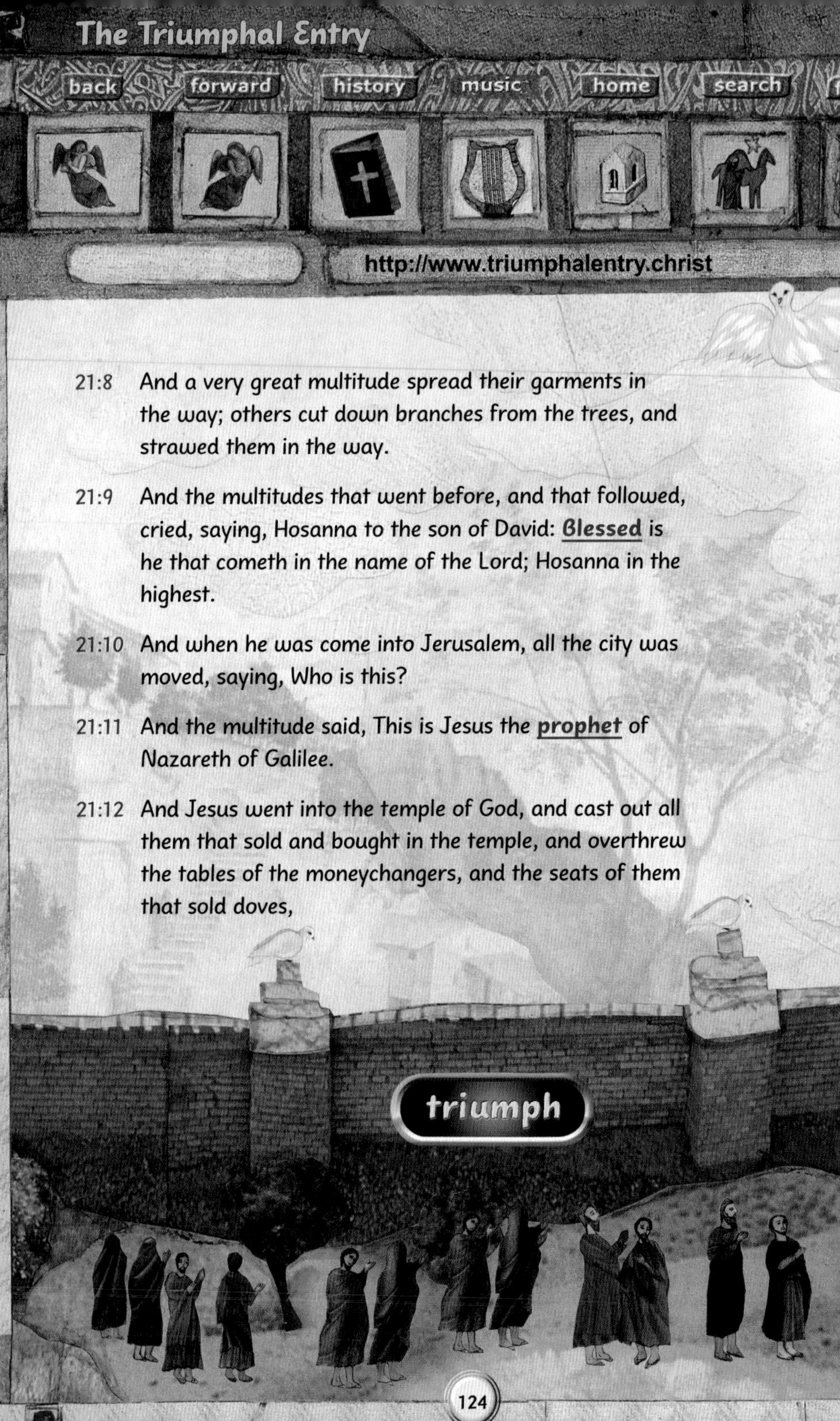

21:8 And a very great multitude spread their garments in
the way; others cut down branches from the trees, and
strawed them in the way.

21:9 And the multitudes that went before, and that followed,
cried, saying, Hosanna to the son of David: **Blessed** is
he that cometh in the name of the Lord; Hosanna in the
highest.

21:10 And when he was come into Jerusalem, all the city was
moved, saying, Who is this?

21:11 And the multitude said, This is Jesus the **prophet** of
Nazareth of Galilee.

21:12 And Jesus went into the temple of God, and cast out all
them that sold and bought in the temple, and overthrew
the tables of the moneychangers, and the seats of them
that sold doves,

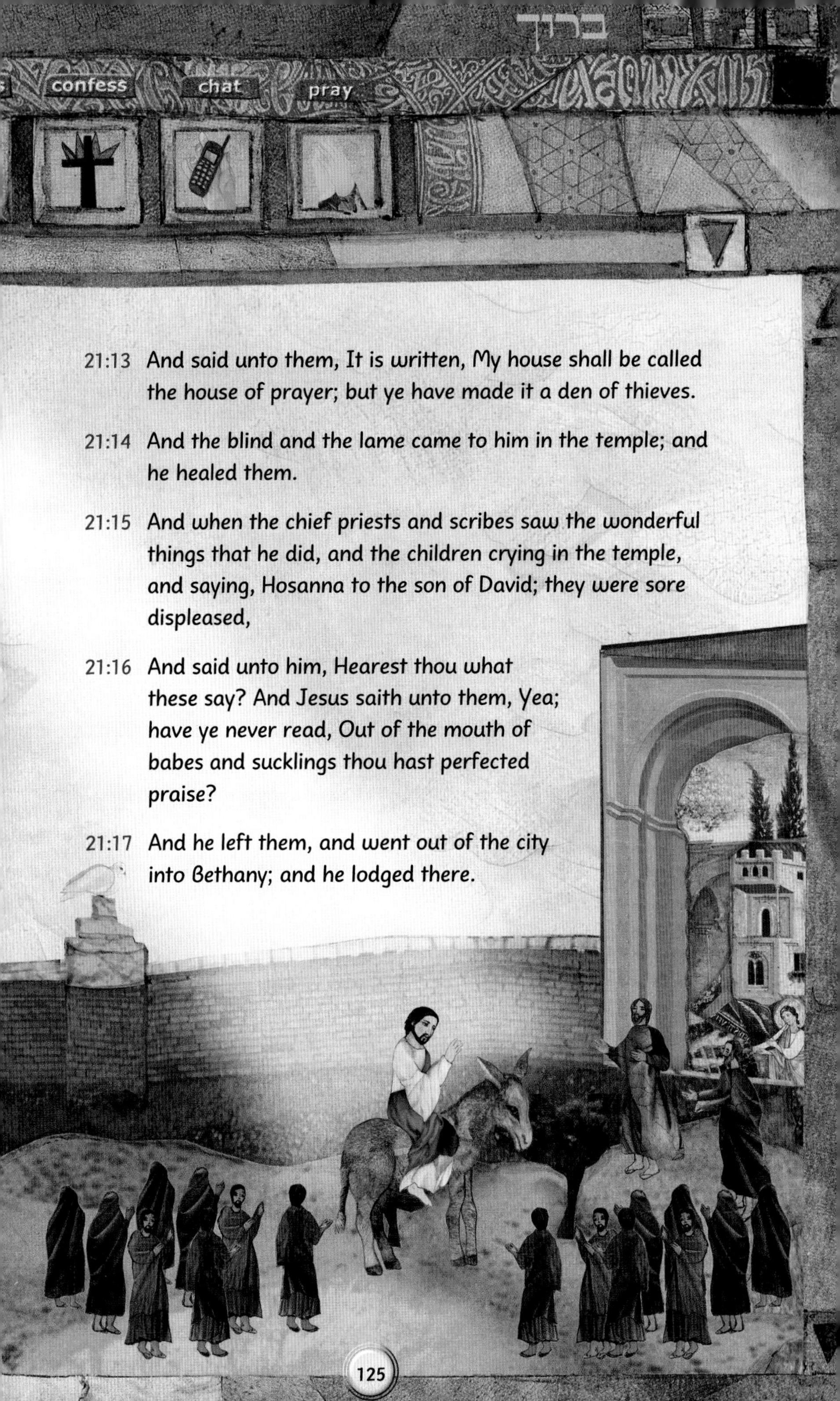

21:13 And said unto them, It is written, My house shall be called the house of prayer; but ye have made it a den of thieves.

21:14 And the blind and the lame came to him in the temple; and he healed them.

21:15 And when the chief priests and scribes saw the wonderful things that he did, and the children crying in the temple, and saying, Hosanna to the son of David; they were sore displeased,

21:16 And said unto him, Hearest thou what these say? And Jesus saith unto them, Yea; have ye never read, Out of the mouth of babes and sucklings thou hast perfected praise?

21:17 And he left them, and went out of the city into Bethany; and he lodged there.

Withering Doubts

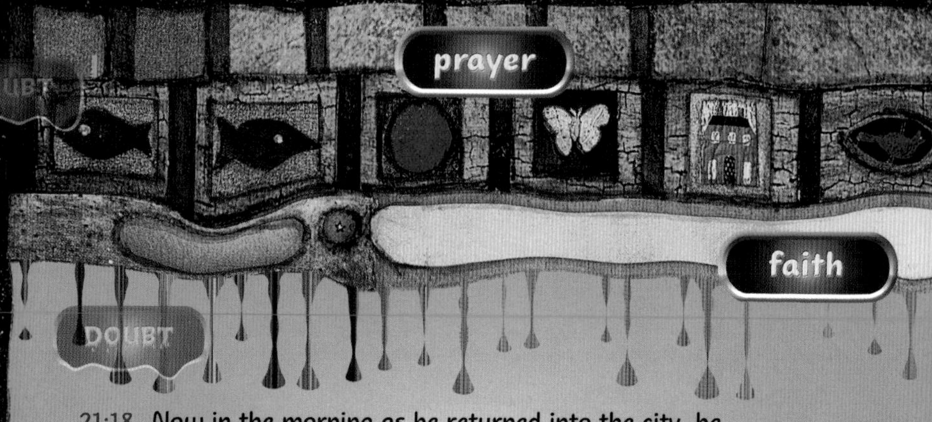

21:18 Now in the morning as he returned into the city, he hungered.

21:19 And when he saw a fig tree in the way, he came to it, and found nothing thereon, but leaves only, and said unto it, Let no fruit grow on thee henceforward for ever. And presently the fig tree withered away.

21:20 And when the disciples saw it, they marvelled, saying, How soon is the fig tree withered away!

21:21 Jesus answered and said unto them, Verily I say unto you, If ye have faith, and doubt not, ye shall not only do this which is done to the fig tree, but also if ye shall say unto this mountain, Be thou removed, and be thou cast into the sea; it shall be done.

21:22 And all things, whatsoever ye shall ask in prayer, believing, ye shall receive.

21:23 And when he was come into the temple, the chief priests and the elders of the people came unto him as he was teaching, and said, By what authority doest thou these things? and who gave thee this authority?

21:24 And Jesus answered and said unto them, I also will ask you one thing, which if ye tell me, I in like wise will tell you by what authority I do these things.

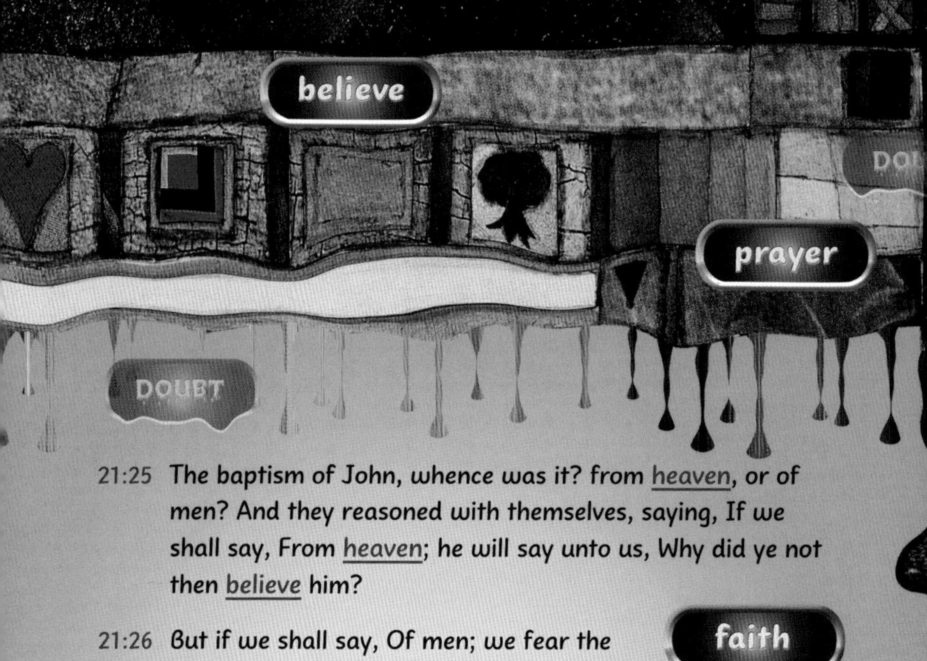

21:25 The baptism of John, whence was it? from heaven, or of
men? And they reasoned with themselves, saying, If we
shall say, From heaven; he will say unto us, Why did ye not
then believe him?

21:26 But if we shall say, Of men; we fear the
people; for all hold John as a prophet.

faith

21:27 And they answered Jesus, and said, We cannot tell. And he
said unto them, Neither tell I you by what authority I do
these things.

21:28 But what think ye? A certain man had two sons; and he
came to the first, and said, Son, go work to day in my
vineyard.

DOUBT

21:29 He answered and said, I will not: but
afterward he repented, and went.

DOUBT

21:30 And he came to the second, and said likewise.
And he answered and said, I go, sir: and went not.

21:31 Whether of them twain did the will of his father?
They say unto him, The first. Jesus saith unto them,
Verily I say unto you, That the publicans and the
harlots go into the kingdom of God before you.

DOUBT

believe

21:32 For John came unto you in the
way of righteousness, and ye believed
him not: but the publicans and the
harlots believed him: and ye, when ye had seen
it, repented not afterward, that ye might believe him.

21:33 Hear another parable: There was a certain householder, which planted a vineyard, and hedged it round about, and digged a winepress in it, and built a tower, and let it out to husbandmen, and went into a far country:

21:34 And when the time of the fruit drew near, he sent his servants to the husbandmen, that they might receive the fruits of it.

21:35 And the husbandmen took his servants, and beat one, and killed another, and stoned another.

21:36 Again, he sent other servants more than the first: and they did unto them likewise.

21:37 But last of all he sent unto them his son, saying, They will ***reverence*** my son.

21:38 But when the husbandmen saw the son, they said among themselves, This is the heir; come, let us kill him, and let us seize on his inheritance.

21:39 And they caught him, and cast him out of the vineyard, and slew him.

21:40 When the lord therefore of the vineyard cometh, what will he do unto those husbandmen?

21:41 They say unto him, He will miserably destroy those wicked men, and will let out his vineyard unto other husbandmen, which shall render him the fruits in their seasons.

21:42 Jesus saith unto them, Did ye never read in the scriptures, The stone which the builders rejected, the same is become the head of the corner: this is the Lord's doing, and it is **marvellous in our eyes**?

21:43 Therefore say I unto you, The kingdom of God shall be taken from you, and given to a nation bringing forth the fruits thereof.

21:44 And whosoever shall fall on this stone shall be broken: but on whomsoever it shall fall, it will grind him to powder.

21:45 And when the chief priests and Pharisees had heard his parables, they perceived that he spake of them.

21:46 But when they sought to lay hands on him, they feared the multitude, because they took him for a prophet.

22:1 And Jesus answered and spake unto them again by parables, and said,

22:2 The kingdom of heaven is like unto a certain king, which made a marriage for his son,

22:3 And sent forth his servants to call them that were bidden to the wedding: and they would not come.

22:4 Again, he sent forth other servants, saying, Tell them which are bidden, Behold, I have prepared my dinner: my oxen and my fatlings are killed, and all things are ready: come unto the marriage.

22:5 But they made light of it, and went their ways, one to his farm, another to his merchandise:

22:6 And the remnant took his servants, and entreated them spitefully, and slew them.

22:7 But when the king heard thereof, he was wroth: and he sent forth his armies, and destroyed those murderers, and burned up their city.

22:8 Then saith he to his servants, The wedding is **ready**, but
they which were bidden were not **worthy**.

22:9 Go ye therefore into the highways, and as many as ye shall
find, bid to the marriage.

22:10 So those servants went out into the highways, and
gathered together all as many as they found, both bad and
good: and the wedding was furnished with guests.

22:11 And when the king came in to see the guests, he saw there
a man which had not on a wedding garment:

22:12 And he saith unto him, Friend, how camest thou in
hither not having a wedding garment? And he was
speechless.

22:13 Then said the king to the servants, Bind
him hand and foot, and take him away,
and cast him into outer darkness,
there shall be weeping and gnashing of
teeth.

22:14 **For many are called, but
few are chosen.**

22:15 Then went the Pharisees, and took
counsel how they might entangle him in
his talk.

22:16 And they sent out unto him their disciples with the
Herodians, saying, Master, we know that thou art true,
and teachest the way of God in truth, neither carest thou
for any man: for thou regardest not the person of men.

22:17 Tell us therefore, What thinkest thou? Is it lawful to give
tribute unto Caesar, or not?

22:18 But Jesus perceived their wickedness, and said, Why tempt
ye me, ye hypocrites?

22:19 Shew me the tribute money. And they brought unto him a
penny.

22:20 And he saith unto them, Whose is this image and
superscription?

22:21 They say unto him, Caesar's. Then saith he unto them,
**Render therefore unto Caesar the things which are
Caesar's; and unto God the things that are God's.**

22:22 When they had heard these words, they marvelled, and left
him, and went their way.

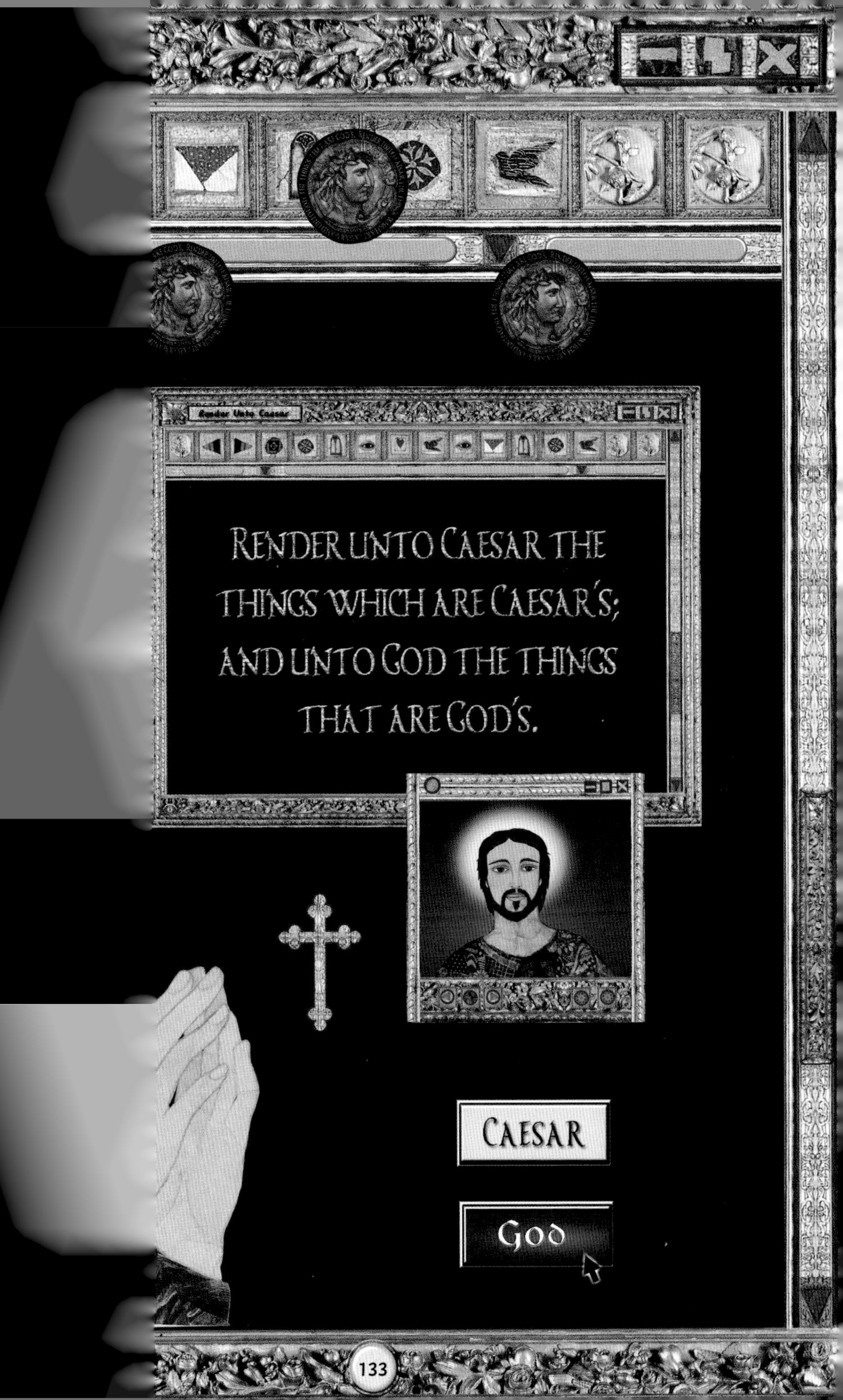
Render Unto Caesar
Render unto Caesar the things which are Caesar's; and unto God the things that are God's.
Caesar
God

THOU SHALT LOVE THE LORD THY GOD WITH ALL THY HEART, AND WITH ALL THY SOUL, AND WITH ALL THY MIND.

http://www.twocommandments.chris

22:23 The same
day came to him the
Sadducees, which say that
there is no resurrection, and asked him,

22:24 Saying, Master, Moses said, If a man die, having no children, his brother shall marry his wife, and raise up seed unto his brother.

22:25 Now there were with us seven brethren: and the first, when he had married a wife, deceased, and, having no issue, left his wife unto his brother:

22:26 Likewise the second also, and the third, unto the seventh.

22:27 And last of all the woman died also.

22:28 Therefore in the resurrection whose wife shall she be of the seven? for they all had her.

22:29 Jesus answered and said unto them, Ye do err, not knowing the scriptures, nor **the power of God**.

22:30 For in the resurrection they neither marry, nor are given in marriage, but are as the angels of God in heaven.

22:31 But as touching the resurrection of the dead, have ye not read that which was spoken unto you by God, saying,

THOU SHALT LOVE THY NEIGHBOUR AS THYSELF.

22:32 I am the God of Abraham, and the God of Isaac, and the God of Jacob? God is not the God of the dead, but of the living.

22:33 And when the multitude heard this, they were astonished at his doctrine.

22:34 But when the Pharisees had heard that he had put the Sadducees to silence, they were gathered together.

22:35 Then one of them, which was a lawyer, asked him a question, tempting him, and saying,

22:36 Master, which is the great commandment in the law?

22:37 Jesus said unto him, **Thou shalt love the Lord thy God with all thy heart, and with all thy soul, and with all thy mind.**

22:38 This is the first and great commandment.

22:39 And the second is like unto it, **Thou shalt love thy neighbour as thyself.**

22:40 On these two commandments hang all the law and the prophets.

Matthew 23:12

22:41 While the Pharisees were gathered together, Jesus asked them,

22:42 Saying, What think ye of Christ? whose son is he? They say unto him, The son of David.

22:43 He saith unto them, How then doth David in spirit call him Lord, saying,

22:44 The LORD said unto my Lord, Sit thou on my right hand, till I make thine enemies thy footstool?

22:45 If David then call him Lord, how is he his son?

22:46 And no man was able to answer him a word, neither durst any man from that day forth ask him any more questions.

23:1 Then spake Jesus to the multitude, and to his disciples,

23:2 Saying The scribes and the Pharisees sit in Moses' seat:

23:3 All therefore whatsoever they bid you observe, that observe and do; but do not ye after their works: for they say, and do not.

23:4 For they bind heavy burdens and grievous to be borne, and lay them on men's shoulders; but they themselves will not move them with one of their fingers.

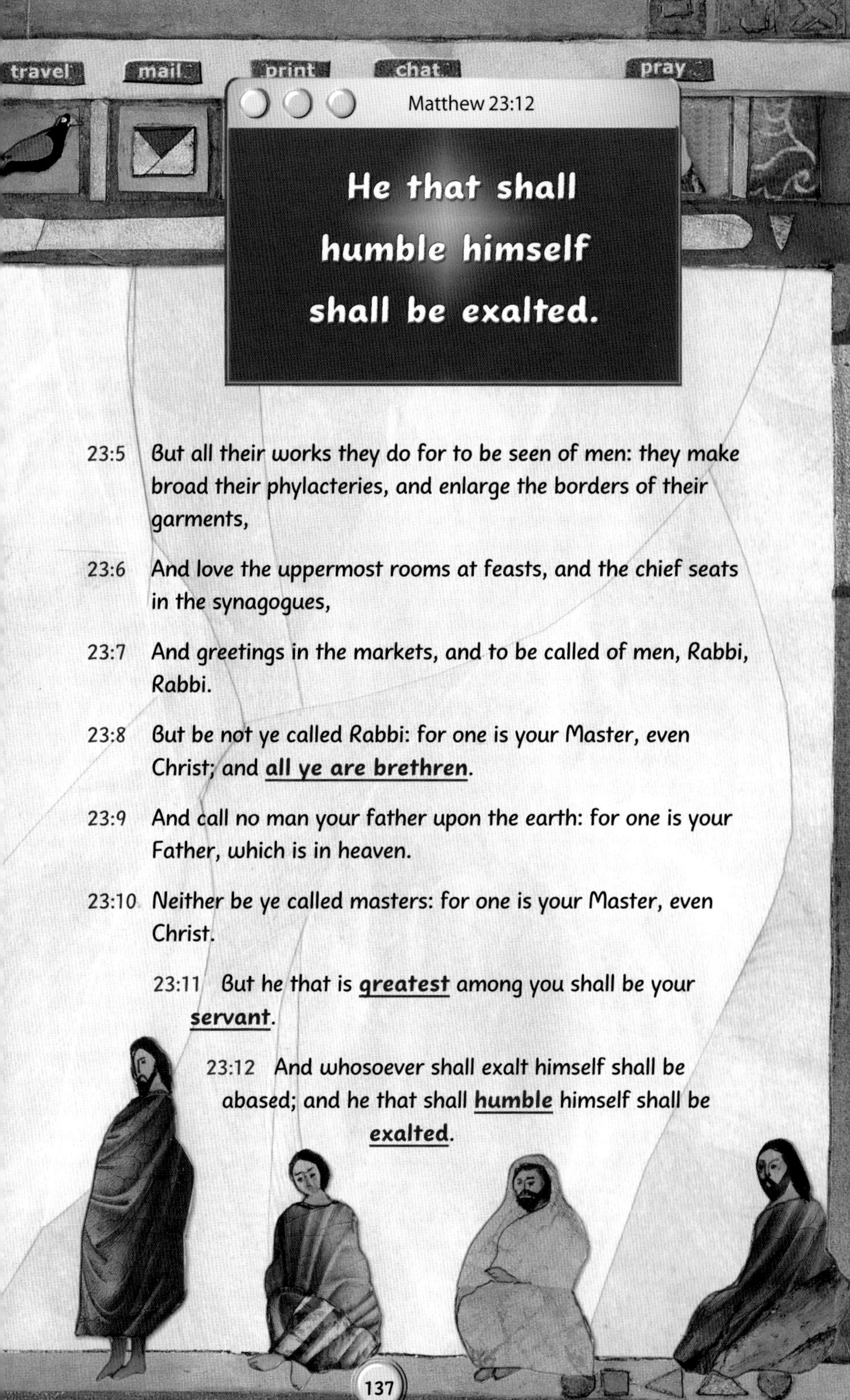
travel
mail
print
chat
pray
Matthew 23:12
He that shall humble himself shall be exalted.

23:5 But all their works they do for to be seen of men: they make broad their phylacteries, and enlarge the borders of their garments,

23:6 And love the uppermost rooms at feasts, and the chief seats in the synagogues,

23:7 And greetings in the markets, and to be called of men, Rabbi, Rabbi.

23:8 But be not ye called Rabbi: for one is your Master, even Christ; and **all ye are brethren**.

23:9 And call no man your father upon the earth: for one is your Father, which is in heaven.

23:10 Neither be ye called masters: for one is your Master, even Christ.

23:11 But he that is **greatest** among you shall be your **servant**.

23:12 And whosoever shall exalt himself shall be abased; and he that shall **humble** himself shall be **exalted**.

23:13 But woe unto you, scribes and Pharisees, hypocrites! for ye shut up the kingdom of heaven against men: for ye neither go in yourselves, neither suffer ye them that are entering to go in.

23:14 Woe unto you, scribes and Pharisees, ***hypocrites!*** for ye devour widows' houses, and for a pretence make long prayer: therefore ye shall receive the greater ***damnation***.

23:15 Woe unto you, scribes and Pharisees, ***hypocrites!*** for ye compass sea and land to make one proselyte, and when he is made, ye make him twofold more the child of hell than yourselves.

23:16 Woe unto you, ye ***blind*** guides, which say, Whosoever shall swear by the temple, it is nothing; but whosoever shall swear by the gold of the temple, he is a debtor!

23:17 Ye ***fools*** and ***blind:*** for whether is greater, the gold, or the temple that sanctifieth the gold?

23:18 And, Whosoever shall swear by the altar, it is nothing; but whosoever sweareth by the gift that is upon it, he is guilty.

23:19 Ye ***fools*** and ***blind:*** for whether is greater, the gift, or the altar that sanctifieth the gift?

23:20 Whoso therefore shall swear by the altar, sweareth by it, and by all things thereon.

23:21 And whoso shall swear by the temple, sweareth by it,
and by him that dwelleth therein.

23:22 And he that shall swear by heaven, sweareth by the
throne of God, and by him that sitteth thereon.

23:23 Woe unto you, scribes and Pharisees, hypocrites! for
ye pay tithe of mint and anise and cummin, and have
omitted the weightier matters of the law, **judgment**,
mercy, and **faith**: these ought ye to have done, and not
to leave the other undone.

23:24 Ye ***blind*** guides, which strain at a gnat, and swallow
a camel.

A Morality Out of Focus

23:25 Woe unto you, scribes and Pharisees, hypocrites! for ye make clean the outside of the cup and of the platter, but within they are full of extortion and excess.

23:26 Thou blind Pharisee, **cleanse first that which is within** the cup and platter, that the outside of them may be clean also.

23:27 Woe unto you, scribes and Pharisees, hypocrites! for ye are like unto whited sepulchres, which indeed appear **beautiful** outward, but are **within** full of dead men's bones, and of all uncleanness.

23:28 Even so ye also outwardly appear **righteous** unto men, but **within** ye are full of hypocrisy and iniquity.

23:29 Woe unto you, scribes and Pharisees, hypocrites! because ye build the tombs of the prophets, and garnish the sepulchres of the righteous,

23:30 And say, If we had been in the days of our fathers, we would not have been partakers with them in the blood of the prophets.

23:31 Wherefore ye be witnesses unto yourselves, that ye are the children of them which killed the prophets.

23:32 Fill ye up then the measure of your fathers.

23:33 Ye serpents, ye generation of vipers, how can ye escape the damnation of hell?

ברוך הבא בשם יהוה

23:34 Wherefore, behold, I send unto you prophets, and wise men, and scribes: and some of them ye shall kill and crucify; and some of them shall ye scourge in your synagogues, and persecute them from city to city:

23:35 That upon you may come all the righteous blood shed upon the earth, from the blood of righteous Abel unto the blood of Zacharias son of Barachias, whom ye slew between the temple and the altar.

23:36 Verily I say unto you, All these things shall come upon this generation.

23:37 O Jerusalem, Jerusalem, thou that killest the prophets, and stonest them which are sent unto thee, how often would I have gathered thy children together, even as a hen gathereth her chickens under her wings, and ye would not!

23:38 Behold, your house is left unto you desolate.

23:39 For I say unto you, Ye shall not see me henceforth, till ye shall say, Blessed is he that cometh in the name of the Lord.

24:1 And Jesus went out, and departed from the temple: and his disciples came to him for to shew him the buildings of the temple.

24:2 And Jesus said unto them, See ye not all these things? verily I say unto you, There shall not be left here one stone upon another, that shall not be thrown down.

24:3 And as he sat upon the mount of Olives, the disciples came unto him privately, saying, Tell us, when shall these things be? and what shall be the sign of thy coming, and of the end of the world?

24:4 And Jesus answered and said unto them, Take heed that no man deceive you.

24:5 For many shall come in my name, saying, I am Christ; and shall deceive many.

24:6 And ye shall hear of wars and rumours of wars: see that ye be not troubled: for all these things must come to pass, but the end is not yet.

WARNING

24:7 For nation shall rise against nation, and kingdom against kingdom: and there shall be famines, and pestilences, and earthquakes, in divers places.

24:8 All these are the beginning of sorrows.

24:9 Then shall they deliver you up to be afflicted, and shall kill you: and ye shall be hated of all nations for my name's sake.

24:10 And then shall many be offended, and shall betray one another, and shall hate one another.

24:11 And many false prophets shall rise, and shall deceive many.

24:12 And because iniquity shall abound, the love of many shall wax cold.

24:13 But he that shall endure unto the end, the same shall be saved.

24:14 And this gospel of the kingdom shall be preached in all the world for a witness unto all nations; and then shall the end come.

24:15 When ye therefore shall see the **ABOMINATION OF DESOLATION**, spoken of by Daniel the prophet, stand in the holy place, (whoso readeth, let him understand:)

24:16 Then let them which be in Judaea flee into the mountains:

24:17 Let him which is on the housetop not come down to take any thing out of his house:

24:18 Neither let him which is in the field return back to take his clothes.

24:19 And woe unto them that are with child, and to them that give suck in those days!

24:20 But pray ye that your flight be not in the winter, neither on the sabbath day:

24:21 For then shall be **GREAT TRIBULATION**, such as was not since the beginning of the world to this time, no, nor ever shall be.

24:22 And except those days should be shortened, there should no flesh be saved: but for the elect's sake those days shall be shortened.

24:23 Then if any man shall say unto you, Lo, here is Christ, or there; believe it not.

24:24 For there shall arise **FALSE** Christs, and **FALSE** prophets, and shall shew great signs and wonders; insomuch that, if it were possible, they shall **DECEIVE** the very elect.

24:25 Behold, I have told you before.

24:26 Wherefore if they shall say unto you, Behold, he is in the desert; go not forth: behold, he is in the secret chambers; **BELIEVE IT NOT**.

24:27 For as the lightning cometh out of the east, and shineth even unto the west; so shall also the coming of the Son of man be.

24:28 For wheresoever the carcase is, there will the eagles be gathered together.

24:29 Immediately after the tribulation of those days shall the sun be **DARKENED**, and the moon shall not give her light, and the stars shall **FALL** from heaven, and the powers of the heavens shall be **SHAKEN**:

24:30 And then shall appear the sign of the Son of man in heaven: and then shall all the tribes of the earth mourn, and they shall see the Son of man coming in the clouds of heaven with power and great glory.

24:31 And he shall send his angels with a great sound of a trumpet, and they shall gather together his elect from the four winds, from one end of heaven to the other.

24:32 Now learn a parable of the fig tree; When his branch is yet tender, and putteth forth leaves, ye know that summer is nigh:

24:33 So likewise ye, when ye shall see all these things, know that it is near, even at the doors.

24:34 Verily I say unto you, This generation shall not pass, till all these things be fulfilled.

24:35 **Heaven and earth shall pass away, but my words shall not pass away.**

24:36 But of that day and hour knoweth no man, no, not the angels of heaven, but my Father only.

24:37 But as the days of Noe were, so shall also the coming of the Son of man be.

24:38 For as in the days that were before the flood they were eating and drinking, marrying and giving in marriage, until the day that Noe entered into the ark,

24:39 And knew not until the flood came, and took them all away; so shall also the coming of the Son of man be.

24:40 Then shall two be in the field; the one shall be taken, and the other left.

24:41 Two women shall be grinding at the mill; the one shall be taken, and the other left.

24:42 **Watch therefore: for ye know not what hour your Lord doth come.**

24:43 But know this, that if the goodman of the house had known in what watch the thief would come, he would have watched, and would not have suffered his house to be broken up.

24:44 **Therefore be ye also ready**: for in such an hour as ye think not the Son of man cometh.

24:45 Who then is a **faithful** and wise servant, whom his lord hath made ruler over his household, to give them meat in due season?

24:46 **Blessed** is that servant, whom his lord when he cometh shall find so doing.

24:47 Verily I say unto you, That he shall make him ruler over all his goods.

24:48 But and if that evil servant shall say in his heart, My lord delayeth his coming;

24:49 And shall begin to smite his fellowservants, and to eat and drink with the drunken;

24:50 The lord of that servant shall come in a day when he looketh not for him, and in an hour that he is not aware of,

24:51 And shall cut him asunder, and appoint him his portion with the hypocrites: there shall be weeping and gnashing of teeth.

25:1 Then shall the kingdom of **heaven** be likened unto ten virgins, which took their lamps, and went forth to meet the bridegroom.

25:2 And five of them were wise, and five were foolish.

25:3 They that were foolish took their lamps, and took no oil with them:

25:4 But the wise took oil in their vessels with their lamps.

25:5 While the bridegroom tarried, they all slumbered and slept.

25:6 And at midnight there was a cry made, Behold, the bridegroom cometh; go ye out to meet him.

25:7 Then all those virgins arose, and trimmed their lamps.

25:8 And the foolish said unto the wise, Give us of your oil; for our lamps are gone out.

25:9 But the wise answered, saying, Not so; lest there be not enough for us and you: but go ye rather to them that sell, and buy for yourselves.

25:10 And while they went to buy, the bridegroom came; and they that were ready went in with him to the marriage: and the door was shut.

25:11 Afterward came also the other virgins, saying, Lord, Lord, open to us.

25:12 But he answered and said, Verily I say unto you, I know you not.

25:13 **Watch** therefore, for ye know neither the day nor the hour wherein the Son of man cometh.

25:14 For the kingdom of heaven is as a man travelling into a far country, who called his own servants, and delivered unto them his goods.

25:15 And unto one he gave five talents, to another two, and to another one; **to every man according to his several ability**; and straightway took his journey.

25:16 Then he that had received the five talents went and traded with the same, and made them other five talents.

25:17 And likewise he that had received two, he also gained other two.

25:18 But he that had received one went and digged in the earth, and hid his lord's money.

25:19 After a long time the lord of those servants cometh, and reckoneth with them.

25:20 And so he that had received five talents came and brought other five talents, saying, lord, thou deliveredst unto me five talents: behold, I have gained beside them five talents more.

25:21 His lord said unto him, Well done, thou **good** and **faithful**
servant: thou hast been faithful over a few things, I will
make thee ruler over many things: enter thou into the **joy**
of thy lord.

25:22 He also that had received two talents came and said,
Lord, thou deliveredst unto me two talents: behold, I have
gained two other talents beside them.

25:23 His lord said unto him, Well done, good and faithful
servant; thou hast been faithful over a few things, I will
make thee ruler over many things: enter thou into the joy
of thy lord.

25:24 Then he which had received the one talent came and said,
Lord, I knew thee that thou art an hard man, reaping
where thou hast not sown, and gathering where thou hast
not strawed:

25:25 And I was **AFRAID**, and went and **HID** thy talent
in the earth: lo, there thou hast that is thine.

25:26 His lord answered and said unto him, Thou **WICKED** and **SLOTHFUL** servant, thou knewest that I reap where I sowed not, and gather where I have not strawed:

25:27 Thou oughtest therefore to have put my money to the exchangers, and then at my coming I should have received mine own with usury.

25:28 Take therefore the talent from him, and give it unto him which hath ten talents.

25:29 **For unto every one that hath shall be given, and he shall have abundance: but from him that hath not shall be taken away even that which he hath.**

25:30 And cast ye the unprofitable servant into outer darkness: there shall be weeping and gnashing of teeth.

25:31 When the Son of man shall come in his glory, and all the holy angels with him, then shall he sit upon the throne of his glory:

25:32 And before him shall be gathered all nations: and he shall separate them one from another, as a shepherd divideth his sheep from the goats:

25:33 And he shall set the sheep on his right hand, but the goats on the left.

25:34 Then shall the King say unto them on his right hand, **Come, ye blessed of my Father**, inherit the kingdom prepared for you from the foundation of the world:

25:35 For I was an hungred, and **ye gave me meat**: I was thirsty, and **ye gave me drink**: I was a stranger, and **ye took me in**:

25:36 Naked, and **ye clothed me**: I was sick, and **ye visited me**: I was in prison, and **ye came unto me**.

25:37 Then shall the righteous answer him, saying, Lord, when saw we thee an hungred, and fed thee? or thirsty, and gave thee drink?

25:38 When saw we thee a stranger, and took thee in? or naked, and clothed thee?

25:39 Or when saw we thee sick, or in prison, and came unto thee?

enter

25:40 And the King shall answer and say unto them, Verily I say
unto you, Inasmuch as ye have done it unto one of the
least of these my brethren, ye have done it unto me.

25:41 Then shall he say also unto them on the left hand, Depart
from me, ye cursed, into everlasting fire, prepared for the
devil and his angels:

25:42 For I was an hungred, and ye gave me no meat: I was
thirsty, and ye gave me no drink:

25:43 I was a stranger, and ye took me not in: naked, and ye
clothed me not: sick, and in prison, and ye visited me not.

25:44 Then shall they also answer him, saying, Lord, when saw
we thee an hungred, or athirst, or a stranger, or naked, or
sick, or in prison, and did not minister unto thee?

25:45 Then shall he answer them, saying, Verily I say unto you,
Inasmuch as ye did it not to one of the least of these, ye
did it not to me.

25:46 And these shall go away into everlasting punishment: but
the righteous into life eternal.

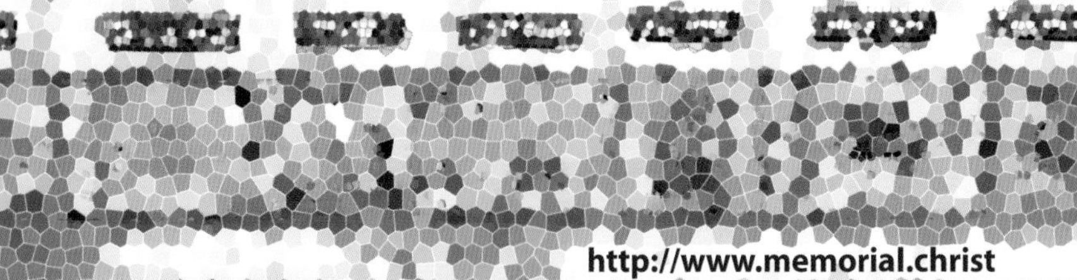

26:1 And it came to pass, when Jesus had finished all these sayings, he said unto his disciples,

26:2 Ye know that after two days is the feast of the passover, and the Son of man is betrayed to be crucified.

26:3 Then assembled together the chief priests, and the scribes, and the elders of the people, unto the palace of the high priest, who was called Caiaphas,

26:4 And consulted that they might take Jesus by subtilty, and kill him.

26:5 But they said, Not on the feast day, lest there be an uproar among the people.

26:6 Now when Jesus was in Bethany, in the house of Simon the leper,

26:7 There came unto him a woman having an alabaster box of very **precious** ointment, and poured it on his head, as he sat at meat.

26:8 But when his disciples saw it, they had indignation, saying, To what purpose is this waste?

26:9 For this ointment might have been sold for much, and given to the poor.

26:10 When Jesus understood it, he said unto them, Why trouble ye the woman? for she hath wrought a **good work** upon me.

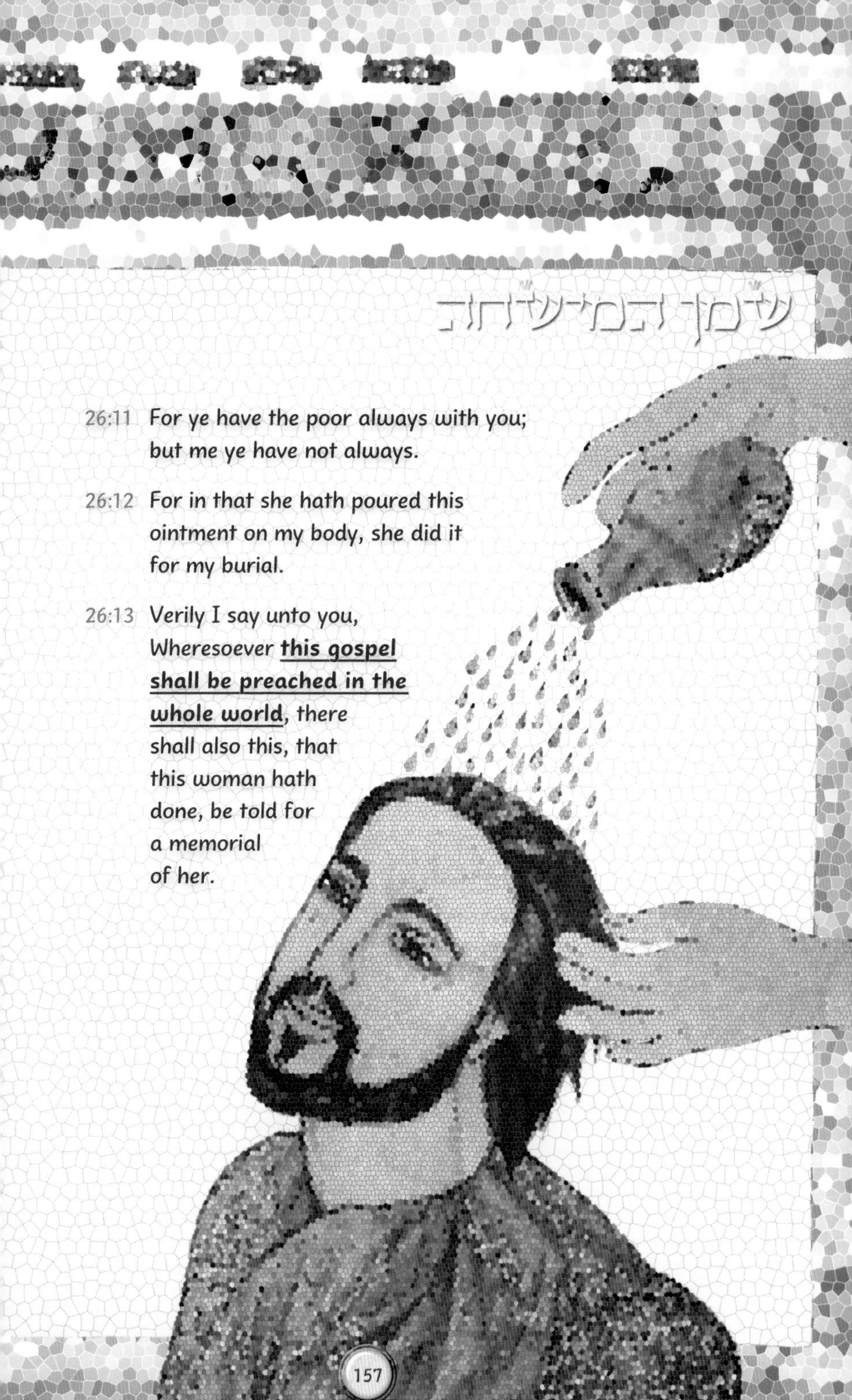

שמן המשחה

26:11 For ye have the poor always with you; but me ye have not always.

26:12 For in that she hath poured this ointment on my body, she did it for my burial.

26:13 Verily I say unto you, Wheresoever **this gospel shall be preached in the whole world**, there shall also this, that this woman hath done, be told for a memorial of her.

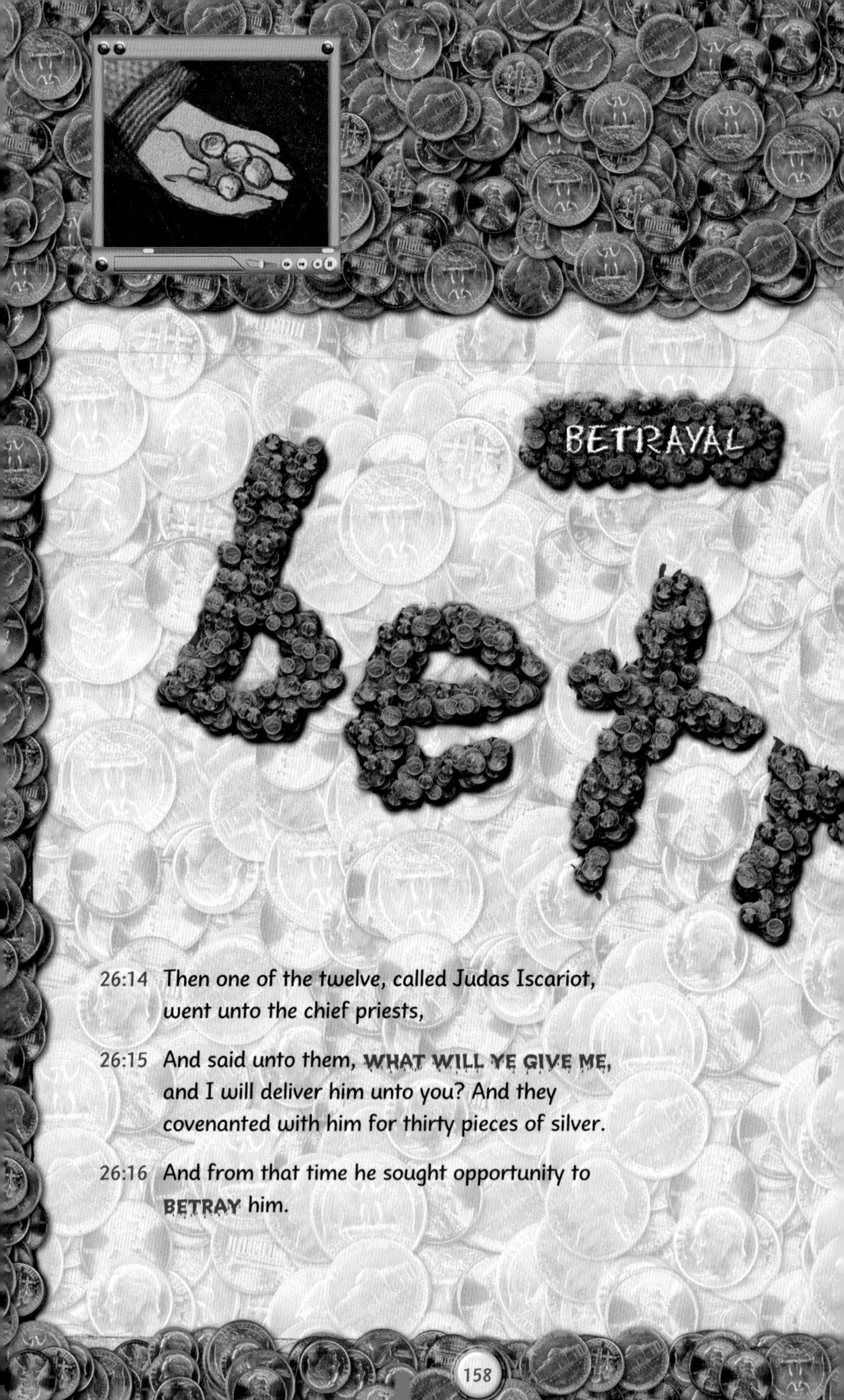

26:14 Then one of the twelve, called Judas Iscariot, went unto the chief priests,

26:15 And said unto them, **WHAT WILL YE GIVE ME,** and I will deliver him unto you? And they covenanted with him for thirty pieces of silver.

26:16 And from that time he sought opportunity to **BETRAY** him.

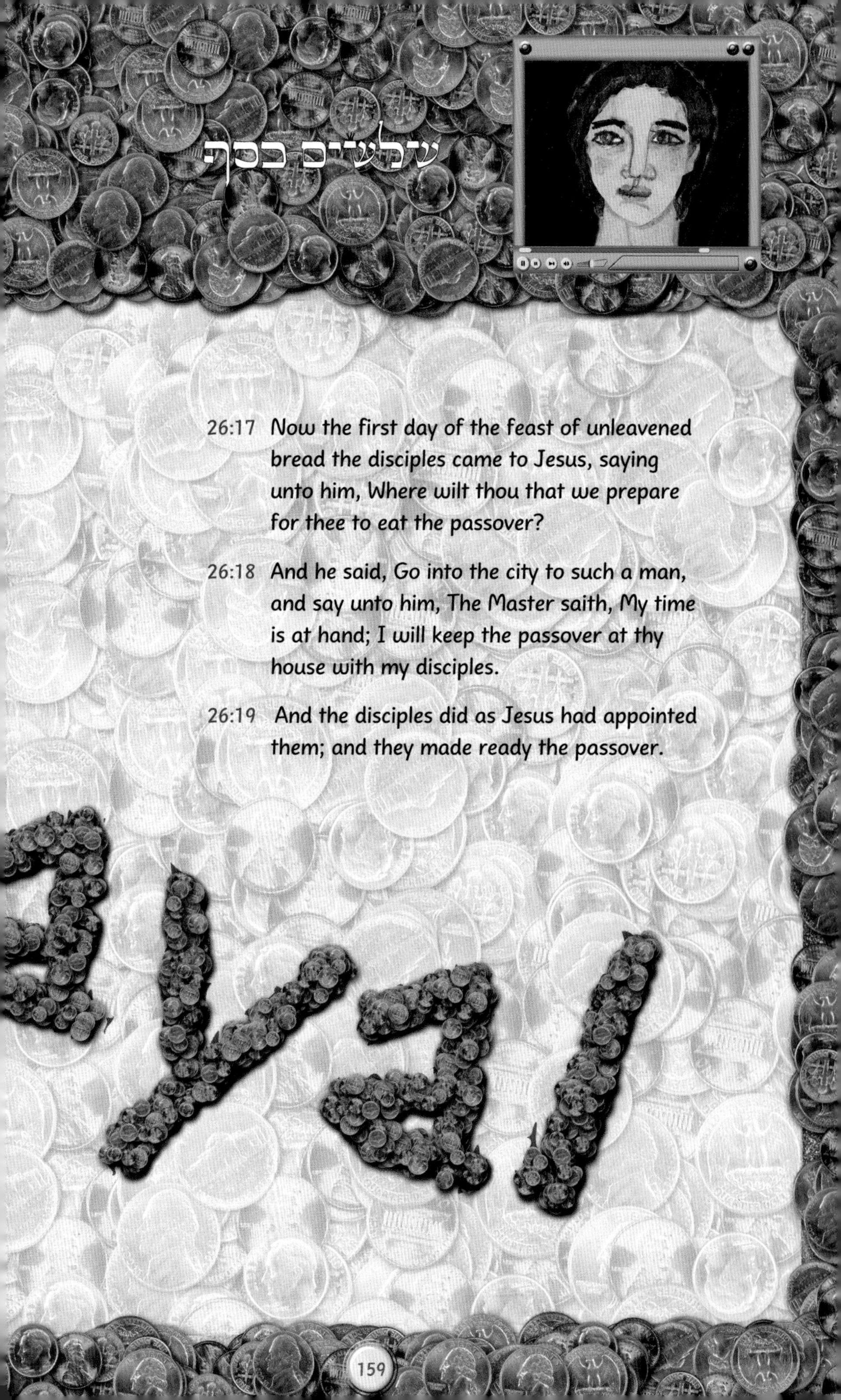

26:17 Now the first day of the feast of unleavened
bread the disciples came to Jesus, saying
unto him, Where wilt thou that we prepare
for thee to eat the passover?

26:18 And he said, Go into the city to such a man,
and say unto him, The Master saith, My time
is at hand; I will keep the passover at thy
house with my disciples.

26:19 And the disciples did as Jesus had appointed
them; and they made ready the passover.

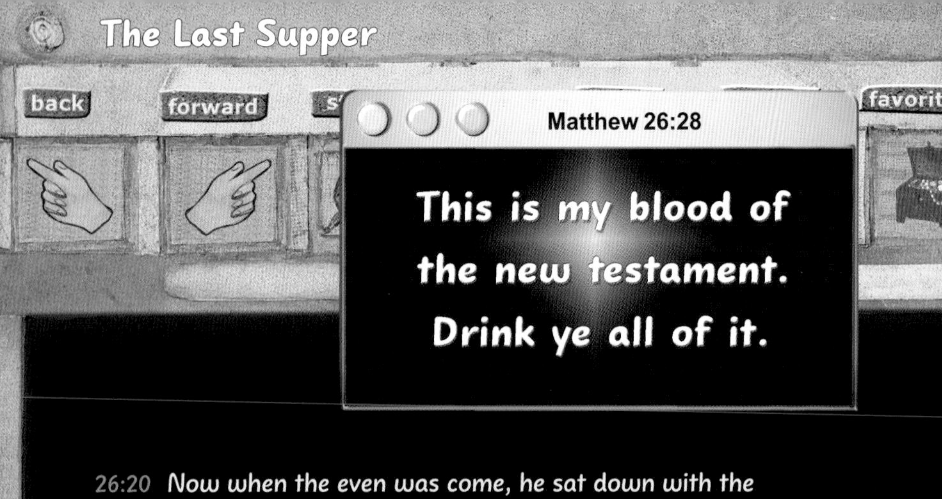

The Last Supper
back
forward
favorite
Matthew 26:28
This is my blood of
the new testament.
Drink ye all of it.

26:20 Now when the even was come, he sat down with the
twelve.

26:21 And as they did eat, he said, Verily I say unto you, that
one of you shall BETRAY me.

26:22 And they were exceeding sorrowful, and began every one
of them to say unto him, Lord, is it I?

26:23 And he answered and said, He that dippeth his hand with
me in the dish, the same shall BETRAY me.

26:24 The Son of man goeth as it is written of him: but WOE
unto that man by whom the Son of man is betrayed! it
had been good for that man if he had not been born.

26:25 Then Judas, which betrayed him, answered and said, Master, is it I? He said unto him, Thou hast said.

26:26 And as they were eating, Jesus took bread, and blessed it, and brake it, and gave it to the disciples, and said, Take, eat; this is my body.

26:27 And he took the cup, and gave thanks, and gave it to them, saying, Drink ye all of it;

26:28 For this is my blood of the new testament, which is shed for many for the remission of sins.

26:29 But I say unto you, I will not drink henceforth of this fruit of the vine, until that day when I drink it new with you in my Father's kingdom.

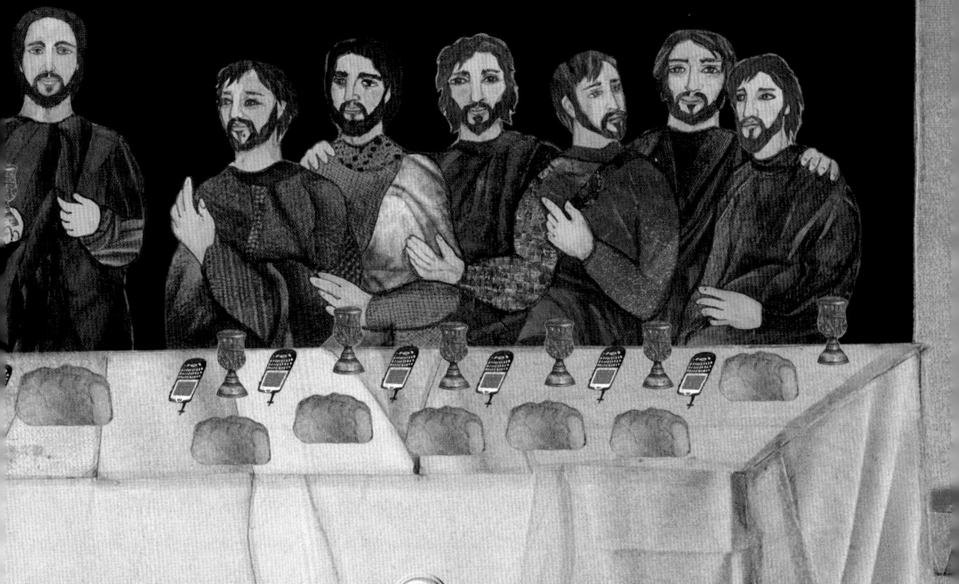

The Sorrowful Soul

26:30 And when they had sung an hymn, they went out into the mount of Olives.

26:31 Then saith Jesus unto them, All ye shall be offended because of me this night: for it is written, I will smite the shepherd, and the sheep of the flock shall be scattered abroad.

26:32 But after I am risen again, I will go before you into Galilee.

26:33 Peter answered and said unto him, Though all men shall be offended because of thee, yet will I never be offended.

26:34 Jesus said unto him, Verily I say unto thee, That this night, before the cock crow, thou shalt deny me thrice.

26:35 Peter said unto him, Though I should die with thee, yet will I not deny thee. Likewise also said all the disciples.

26:36 Then cometh Jesus with them unto a place called Gethsemane, and saith unto the disciples, Sit ye here, while I go and pray yonder.

26:37 And he took with him Peter and the two sons of Zebedee, and began to be sorrowful and very heavy.

26:38 Then saith he unto them, My soul is exceeding sorrowful, even unto death: tarry ye here, and watch with me.

26:39 And he went a little farther, and fell on his face, and prayed, saying, O my Father, if it be possible, let this cup pass from me: nevertheless not as I will, but as thou wilt.

26:40 And he cometh unto the disciples, and findeth them asleep, and saith unto Peter, What, could ye not watch with me one hour?

26:41 Watch and pray, that ye enter not into temptation: the spirit indeed is willing, but the flesh is weak.

26:42 He went away again the second time, and prayed, saying, O my Father, if this cup may not pass away from me, except I drink it, thy will be done.

26:43 And he came and found them asleep again: for their eyes were heavy.

DENY DENY DENY

click to deny

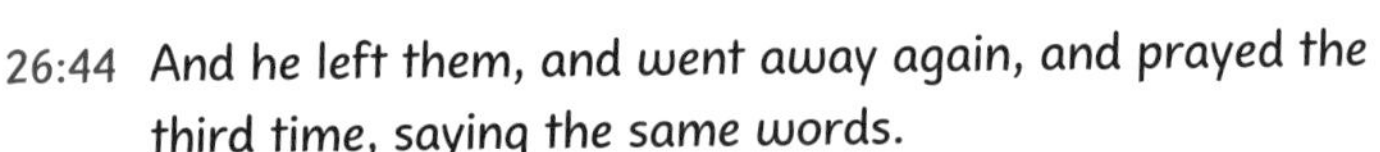

26:44 And he left them, and went away again, and prayed the third time, saying the same words.

26:45 Then cometh he to his disciples, and saith unto them, Sleep on now, and take your rest: behold, the hour is at hand, and the Son of man is betrayed into the hands of sinners.

26:46 Rise, let us be going: behold, he is at hand that doth betray me.

26:47 And while he yet spake, lo, Judas, one of the twelve, came, and with him a great multitude with swords and staves, from the chief priests and elders of the people.

26:48 Now he that betrayed him gave them a sign, saying, Whomsoever I shall kiss, that same is he: hold him fast.

26:49 And forthwith he came to Jesus, and said, Hail, master; and kissed him.

26:50 And Jesus said unto him, Friend, wherefore art thou come? Then came they, and laid hands on Jesus and took him.

26:51 And, behold, one of them which were with Jesus stretched out his hand, and drew his **SWORD**, and **STRUCK** a servant of the high priest's, and **SMOTE** off his ear.

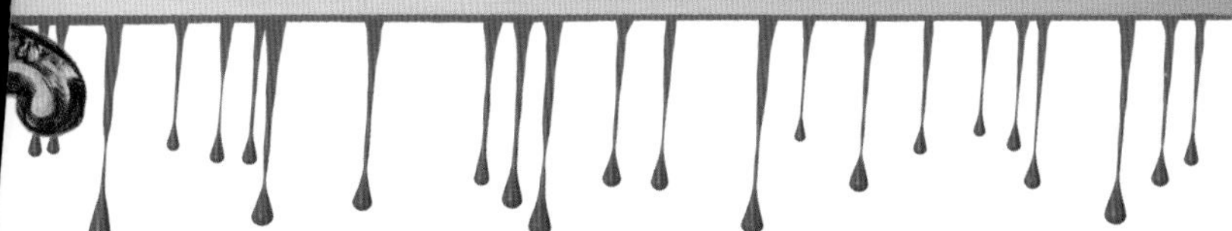

26:52 Then said Jesus unto him, **Put up again thy sword**
into his place: for all they that take the sword
shall perish with the sword.

26:53 Thinkest thou that I cannot now pray to my Father,
and he shall presently give me more than twelve
legions of angels?

26:54 But how then shall the scriptures be fulfilled, that
thus it must be?

26:55 In that same hour said Jesus to the multitudes, Are ye
come out as against a thief with swords and staves
for to take me? I sat daily with you teaching in the
temple, and ye laid no hold on me.

26:56 But all this was done, that the scriptures of the
prophets might be fulfilled. Then all the disciples
forsook him, and fled.

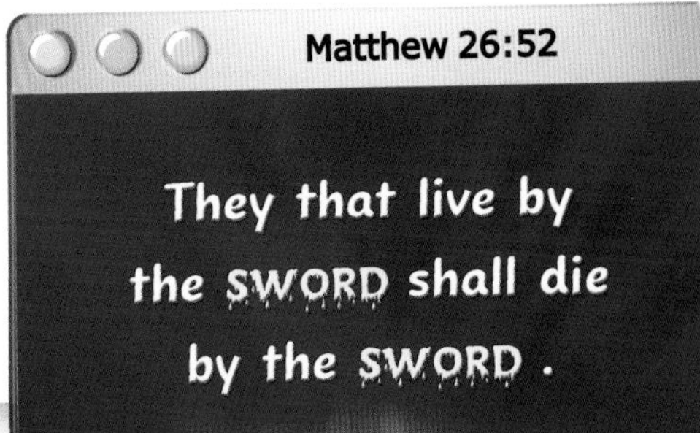
Matthew 26:52
They that live by
the SWORD shall die
by the SWORD .

26:57 And they that had laid hold on Jesus led him away to Caiaphas the high priest, where the scribes and the elders were assembled.

26:58 But Peter followed him afar off unto the high priest's palace, and went in, and sat with the servants, to see the end.

26:59 Now the chief priests, and elders, and all the council, sought **FALSE WITNESS AGAINST JESUS**, to put him to death;

26:60 But found none: yea, though many **FALSE** witnesses came, yet found they none. At the last came two **FALSE** witnesses,

26:61 And said, This fellow said, I am able to **DESTROY** the temple of God, and to build it in three days.

26:62 And the high priest arose, and said unto him, Answerest thou nothing? what is it which these witness against thee?

26:63 But Jesus held his **peace**, And the high priest answered and said unto him, I adjure thee by the **living God**, that thou tell us whether thou be the **Christ**, the Son of God.

26:64 Jesus saith unto him, Thou hast said: nevertheless I say unto you, Hereafter shall ye see the Son of man sitting on the right hand of power, and coming in the clouds of **heaven**.

26:65 Then the high priest rent his clothes, saying, He hath spoken **BLASPHEMY**; what further need have we of witnesses? behold, now ye have heard his **BLASPHEMY**.

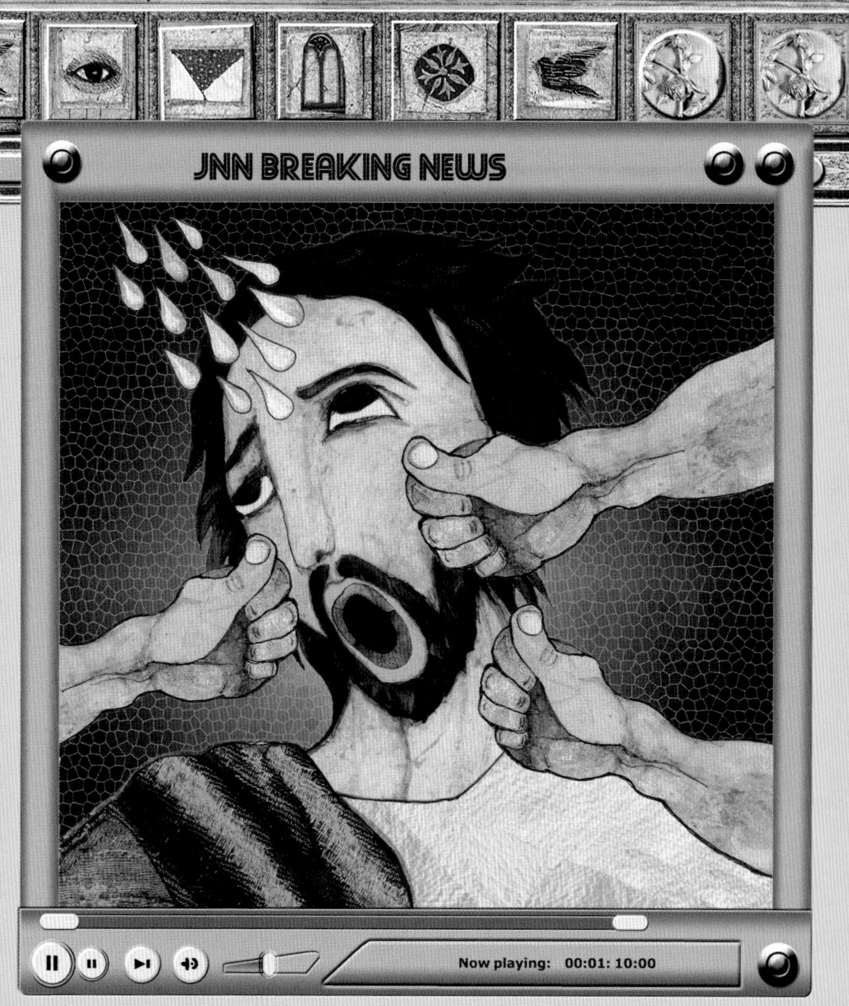

26:66 What think ye? They answered and said, He is **GUILTY** of **DEATH**.

26:67 Then did they **SPIT** in his face, and **BUFFETED** him; and others **SMOTE** him with the palms of their hands,

26:68 Saying, Prophesy unto us, thou Christ, Who is he that smote thee?

26:69 Now Peter sat without in the palace: and a damsel came
unto him, saying, Thou also wast with Jesus of Galilee.

26:70 But he DENIED before them all, saying, I
know not what thou sayest.

REMORSE

26:71 And when he was gone out into the porch,
another maid saw him, and said unto them that were
there, This fellow was also with Jesus of Nazareth.

26:72 And again he denied with an oath, I do not know the man.

26:73 And after a while came unto him they that stood by, and
said to Peter, Surely thou also art one of them; for thy
speech betrayeth thee.

26:74 Then began he to curse and to swear, saying, I know not
the man. And immediately the cock crew.

26:75 And Peter remembered the word of Jesus, which said unto
him, Before the cock crow, thou shalt deny me thrice. And
he went out, and WEPT bitterly.

27:1 When the morning was come, all the chief priests and elders
of the people took counsel against Jesus to put him to
death:

27:2 And when they had bound him, they led him away, and
delivered him to Pontius Pilate the governor.

27:3 Then Judas, which had BETRAYED him, when he saw
that he was condemned, repented himself, and brought
again the thirty pieces of silver to the chief priests and
elders,

27:4 Saying, I HAVE SINNED in that
I have BETRAYED the innocent
BLOOD. And they said, What is
that to us? see thou to that.

27:5 And he cast down the pieces
of silver in the temple, and
departed, and went and
hanged himself.

REMORSE

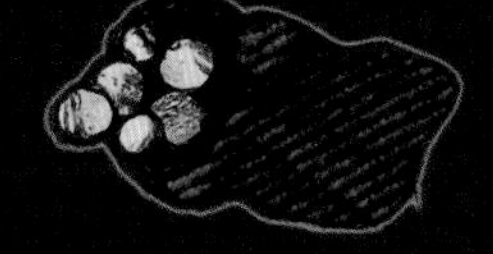

27:6 And the **CHIEF PRIESTS** took the silver pieces, and said, It is not lawful for to put them into the treasury, because it is the **PRICE OF BLOOD**.

27:7 And they took counsel, and bought with them the potter's field, to bury strangers in.

27:8 Wherefore that field was called, The field of **BLOOD**, unto this day.

27:9 Then was fulfilled that which was spoken by Jeremy the prophet, saying, And they took the thirty pieces of silver, the price of him that was valued, whom they of the children of Israel did value;

27:10 And gave them for the potter's field, as the Lord appointed me.

27:11 And Jesus stood before the governor: and the governor asked him, saying, Art thou the King of the Jews? And Jesus said unto him, Thou sayest.

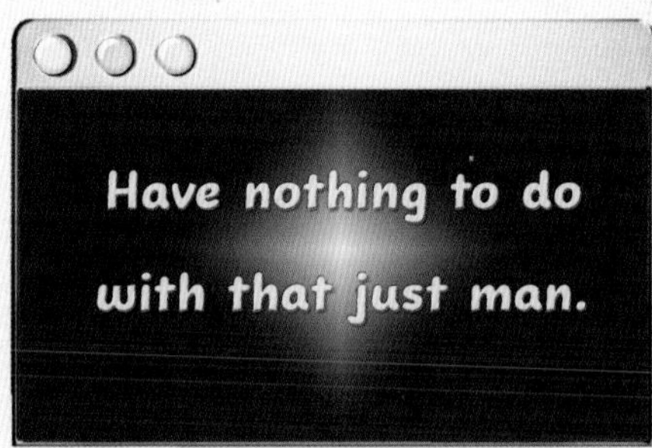

Have nothing to do
with that just man.

27:12 And when he was accused of the **CHIEF PRIESTS** and **ELDERS**, he answered nothing.

27:13 Then said Pilate unto him, Hearest thou not how many things they witness against thee?

27:14 And he answered him to never a word; insomuch that the governor marvelled greatly.

27:15 Now at that feast the governor was wont to release unto the people a prisoner, whom they would.

27:16 And they had then a notable prisoner, called **BARABBAS**.

27:17 Therefore when they were gathered together, Pilate said unto them, Whom will ye that I release unto you? **BARABBAS**, or **Jesus** which is called **Christ**?

27:18 For he knew that for **ENVY** they had delivered him.

27:19 When he was set down on the judgment seat, his wife sent unto him, saying, Have thou nothing to do with that **just** man: for I have **SUFFERED** many things this day in a dream because of him.

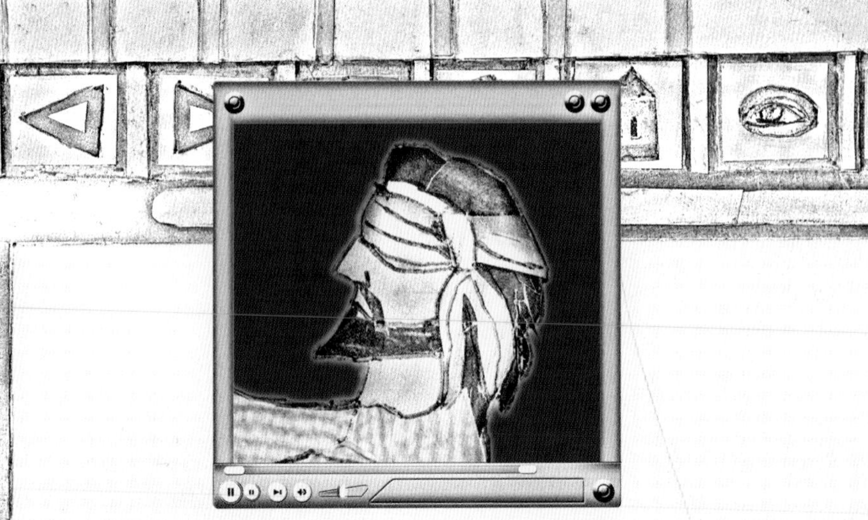

27:20 But the chief priests and elders persuaded the multitude that they should ask Barabbas, and **DESTROY** Jesus.

27:21 The governor answered and said unto them, Whether of the twain will ye that I release unto you? They said, Barabbas.

27:22 Pilate saith unto them, What shall I do then with Jesus which is called Christ? They all say unto him, Let him be **CRUCIFIED**.

27:23 And the governor said, Why, what evil hath he done? But they cried out the more, saying, **LET HIM BE CRUCIFIED**.

27:24 When Pilate saw that he could prevail nothing, but that rather a tumult was made, he took water, and washed his hands before the multitude, saying, I am innocent of the blood of this just person: see ye to it.

27:25 Then answered all the people, and said, His **BLOOD** be on us, and on our children.

27:26 Then released he Barabbas unto them: and when he had scourged Jesus, he delivered him to be **CRUCIFIED**.

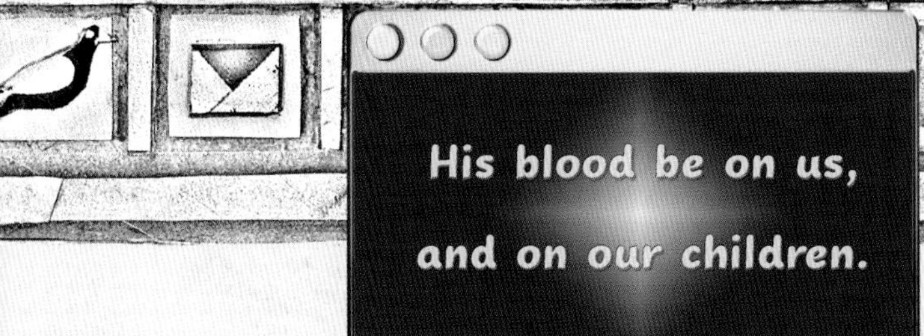
His blood be on us,
and on our children.

27:27 Then the soldiers of the governor took Jesus into the common hall, and gathered unto him the whole band of soldiers.

27:28 And they stripped him, and put on him a scarlet robe.

27:29 And when they had platted a crown of thorns, they put it upon his head, and a reed in his right hand: and they bowed the knee before him, and **MOCKED** him, saying, Hail, King of the Jews!

27:30 And they **SPIT** upon him, and took the reed, and **SMOTE** him on the head.

27:31 And after that they had **MOCKED** him, they took the robe off from him, and put his own raiment on him, and led him away to **CRUCIFY** him.

27:32 And as they came out, they found a man of Cyrene, Simon by name: him they compelled to bear his cross.

CRUCIFY

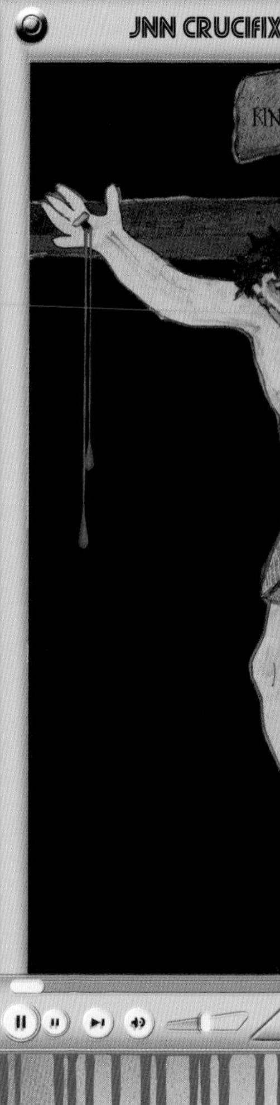

27:33 And when they were come unto a
place called Golgotha, that is to say,
a place of a skull,

27:34 They gave him vinegar to drink
mingled with gall: and when he had
tasted thereof, he would not drink.

27:35 And they CRUCIFIED him, and
parted his garments, casting lots:
that it might be fulfilled which was
spoken by the prophet, They parted
my garments among them, and
upon my vesture did they cast lots.

27:36 And sitting down they watched him there;

27:37 And set up over his head his accusation written, THIS IS JESUS THE KING OF THE JEWS.

27:38 Then were there two thieves CRUCIFIED with him, one on the right hand, and another on the left.

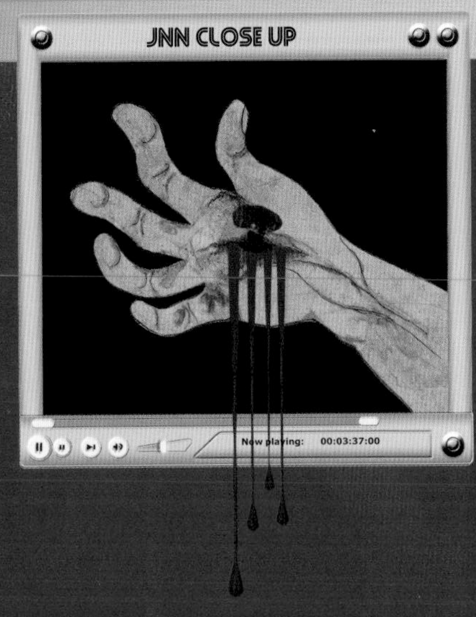

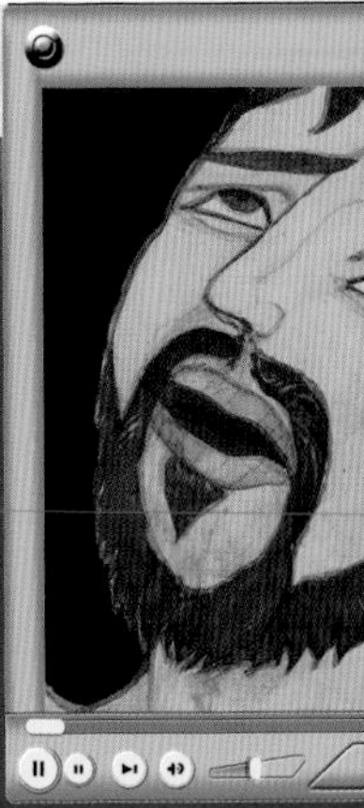

27:39 And they that passed by reviled him, wagging their
heads,

27:40 And saying, Thou that **DESTROYEST** the temple, and
buildest it in three days, save thyself. If thou be the
Son of God, come down from the cross.

27:41 Likewise also the chief priests **MOCKING** him, with
the scribes and elders, said,

crucifixion

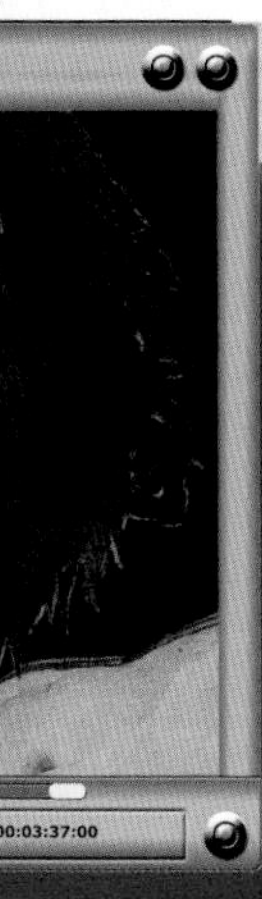

27:42 He saved others; himself he cannot save. If he be
the King of Israel, let him now come down from
the cross, and we will believe him.

27:43 He trusted in God; let him deliver him now, if he
will have him: for he said, I am the Son of God.

27:44 The thieves also, which were CRUCIFIED with him,
cast the same in his teeth.

27:45 Now from the sixth hour there was
darkness over all the land unto the ninth
hour.

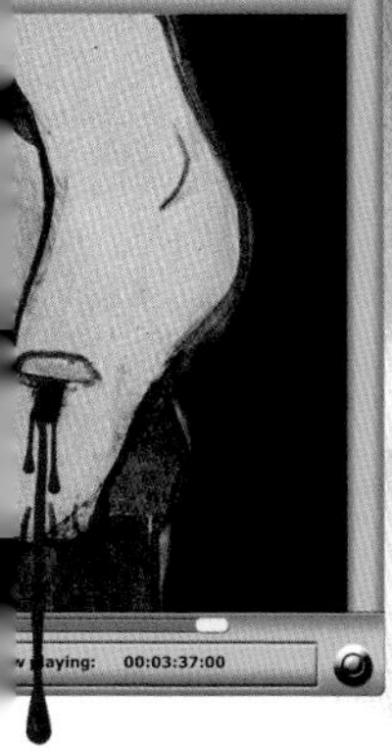

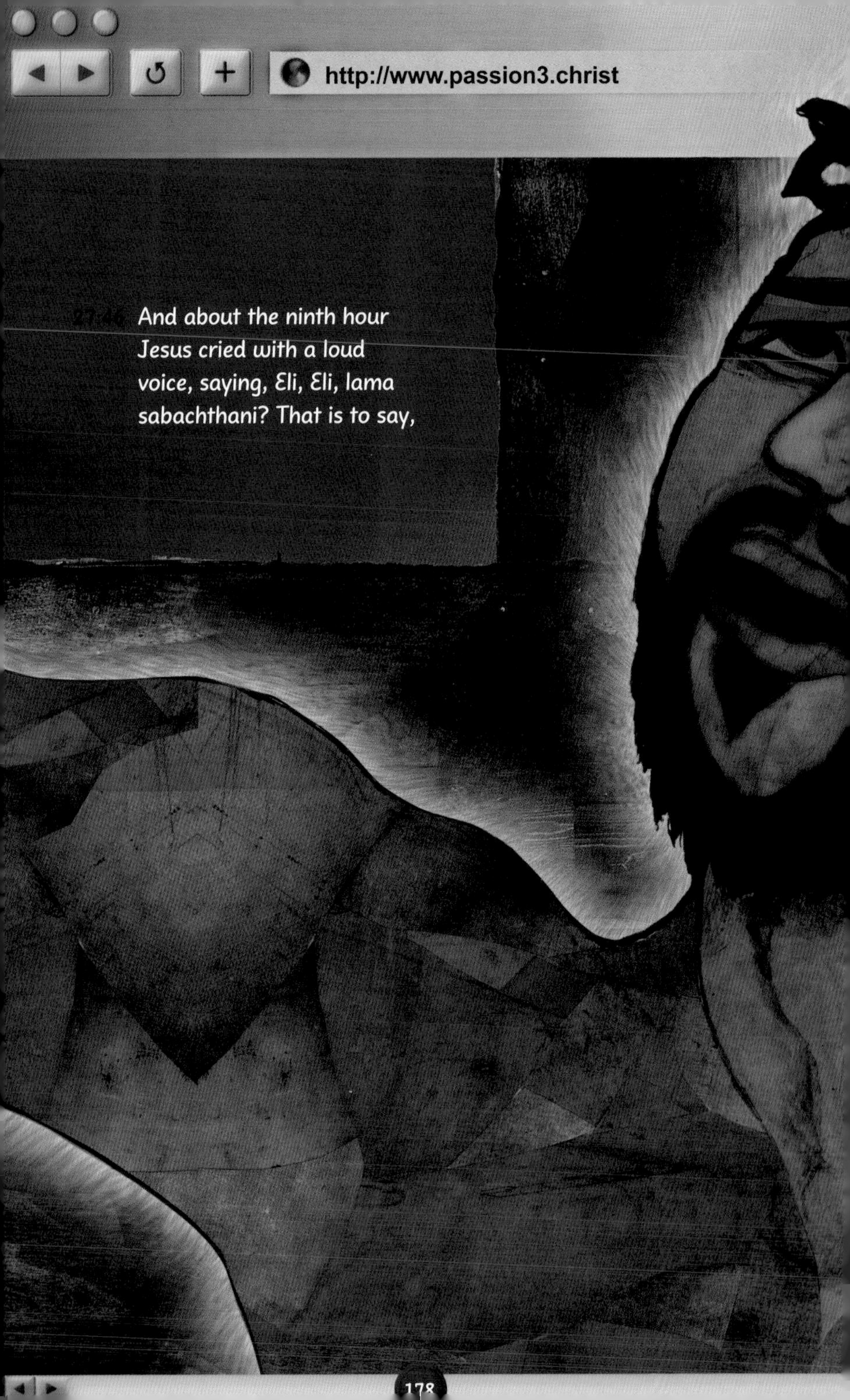

27:46 And about the ninth hour
Jesus cried with a loud
voice, saying, Eli, Eli, lama
sabachthani? That is to say,

in search of God
אלי
אלי
אלי אלי למה שבקתני
My God, my God,
why hast thou
forsaken me?

http://www.earthquake.crucifixion.christ

27:47 Some of them that stood there, when they
heard that, said, This man calleth for Elias.

27:48 And straightway one of them ran, and took a
spunge, and filled it with vinegar, and put it on
a reed, and gave him to drink.

27:49 The rest said, Let be, let us see whether Elias
will come to save him.

27:50 Jesus, when he had cried again with a loud voice,
yielded up the ghost.

27:51 And, behold, the veil of the temple was rent in
twain from the top to the bottom; and the earth
did **QUAKE**, and the rocks rent;

27:52 And the graves were opened; and many bodies
of the saints which slept arose,

Son

27:53 And came out of the graves after his
resurrection, and went into the holy city,
and appeared unto many.
27:54 Now when the centurion, and they that
were with him, watching Jesus, saw the
earthquake, and those things that were
done, they feared greatly, saying, Truly
this was the Son of God.
27:55 And many women were there beholding
afar off, which followed Jesus from Galilee,
ministering unto him:
27:56 Among which was Mary Magdalene, and
Mary the mother of James and Joses, and
the mother of Zebedees children.

The Sealed Sepulchre

27:57 When the even was come, there came a rich man of Arimathaea, named Joseph, who also himself was Jesus' disciple:

27:58 He went to Pilate, and begged the body of Jesus. Then Pilate commanded the body to be delivered.

27:59 And when Joseph had taken the body, he wrapped it in a clean linen cloth,

faith

0 And laid it in his own new tomb, which he had hewn out
in the rock: and he rolled a great stone to the door of the
sepulchre, and departed.

1 And there was Mary Magdalene, and the other Mary,
sitting over against the sepulchre.

2 Now the next day, that followed the day of the
preparation, the chief priests and Pharisees came together
unto Pilate,

3 Saying, Sir, we remember that that deceiver said, while he
was yet alive, After three days I will rise again.

4 Command therefore that the sepulchre be made sure until
the third day, lest his disciples come by night, and steal
him away, and say unto the people, He is risen from the
dead: so the last error shall be worse than the first.

5 Pilate said unto them, Ye have a watch: go your way,
make it as sure as ye can.

6 So they went, and made the sepulchre sure, sealing the
stone, and setting a watch.

28:1 In the end of the sabbath, as it began to dawn toward the first day of the week, came Mary Magdalene and the other Mary to see the sepulchre.

28:2 And, behold, there was a great earthquake: for the **angel** of the Lord descended from **heaven**, and came and rolled back the stone from the door, and sat upon it.

28:3 His countenance was like lightning, and his raiment white as snow:

28:4 And for fear of him the keepers did shake, and became as dead men.

28:5 And the angel answered and said unto the women, Fear not ye: for I know that ye seek Jesus, which was crucified.

28:6 He is not here: for **he is risen**, as he said. Come, see the place where the Lord lay.

28:7 And go quickly, and tell his disciples that **he is risen** from
the dead; and, behold, he goeth before you into Galilee;
there shall ye see him: lo, I have told you.

28:8 And they departed quickly from the sepulchre with fear
and **great joy**; and did run to bring his disciples word.

28:9 And as they went to tell his disciples, behold, Jesus met them, saying, All hail. And they came and held him by the feet, and worshipped him.

28:10 Then said Jesus unto them, **Be not afraid**: go tell my brethren that they go into Galilee, and there shall they **see** me.

28:11 Now when they were going, behold, some of the watch came into the city, and shewed unto the chief priests all the things that were done.

28:12 And when they were assembled with the elders, and had taken counsel, they gave large money unto the soldiers,

28:13 Saying, Say ye, His disciples came by night, and stole him away while we slept.

28:14 And if this come to the governor's ears, we will persuade him, and secure you.

28:15 So they took the money, and did as they were taught: and this saying is commonly reported among the Jews until this day.

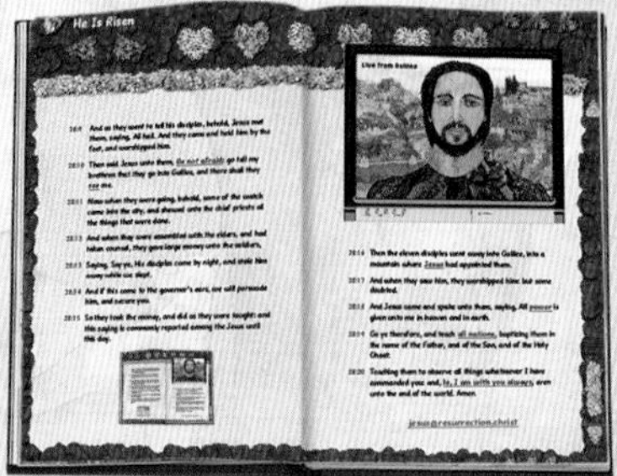

28:16 Then the eleven disciples went away into Galilee, into a mountain where **Jesus** had appointed them.

28:17 And when they saw him, they worshipped him: but some doubted.

28:18 And Jesus came and spake unto them, saying, All **power** is given unto me in heaven and in earth.

28:19 Go ye therefore, and teach **all nations**, baptizing them in the name of the Father, and of the Son, and of the Holy Ghost:

28:20 Teaching them to observe all things whatsoever I have commanded you: and, **lo, I am with you always**, even unto the end of the world. Amen.

jesus@resurrection.christ

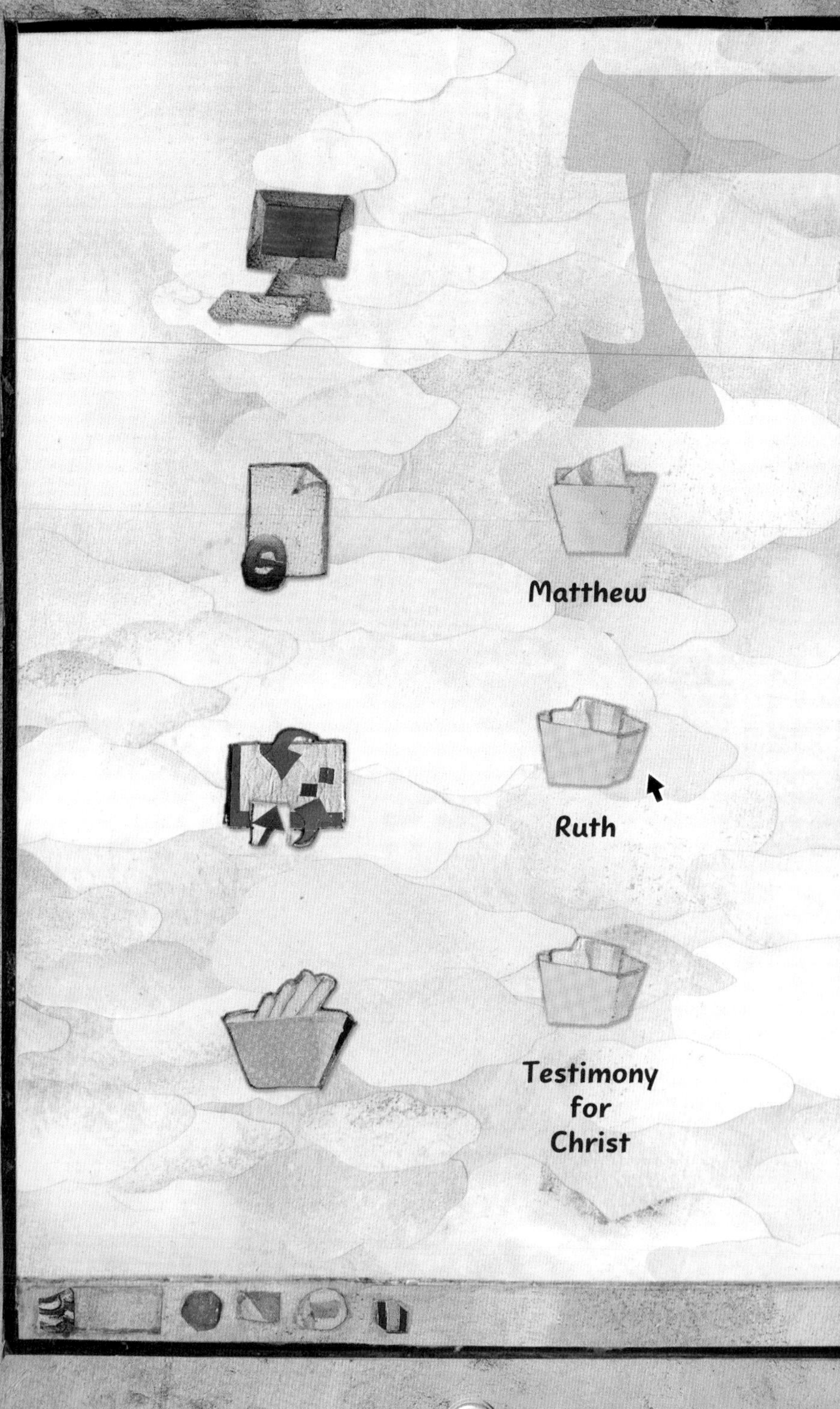
Matthew
Ruth
Testimony
for
Christ

Ruth

turn to enter

1:1 Now it came to pass in the days when the **judges ruled**, that there was a famine in the land. And a certain man of Bethlehemjudah went to sojourn in the country of Moab, he, and his wife, and his two sons.

1:2 And the name of the man was Elimelech, and the name of his wife Naomi, and the name of his two sons Mahlon and Chilion, Ephrathites of Bethlehemjudah. And they came into the country of Moab, and continued there.

1:3 And Elimelech Naomi's husband died; and she was left, and her two sons.

1:4 And they took them wives of the women of Moab; the name of the one was Orpah, and the name of the other **Ruth**: and they dwelled there about ten years.

1:5 And Mahlon and Chilion died also both of them; and the woman was left of her two sons and her husband.

1:6 Then she arose with her daughters in law, that she might return from the country of Moab: for she had heard in the country of Moab how that the LORD had visited his people in giving them bread.

1:7 Wherefore she went forth out of the place where she was, and hertwo daughters in law with her; and they went on the way to return unto the land of Judah.

1:8 And Naomi said unto her two daughters in law, Go, return each to her mother's house: the LORD deal **kindly** with you, as ye have dealt with the dead, and with me.

1:9 The LORD grant you that ye may find rest, each of you in the house of her husband. Then she **kissed** them; and they lifted up their voice, and wept.

1:10 And they said unto her, Surely we will return with thee unto thy people.

1:11 And Naomi said, Turn again, my daughters: why will ye go with me? are there yet any more sons in my womb, that they may be your husbands?

1:12 Turn again, my daughters, go your way; for I am too old to have an husband. If I should say, I have hope, if I should have an husband also to night, and should also bear sons;

1:13 Would ye tarry for them till they were grown? would ye stay for them from having husbands? nay, my daughters; for it grieveth me much for your sakes that the hand of the LORD is gone out against me.

1:14 And they lifted up their voice, and wept again: and Orpah **kissed** her mother in law; but Ruth clave unto her.

1:15 And she said, Behold, thy sister in law is gone back unto her people, and unto her gods: return thou after thy sister in law.

back
forward
stop
refresh
home
favorites

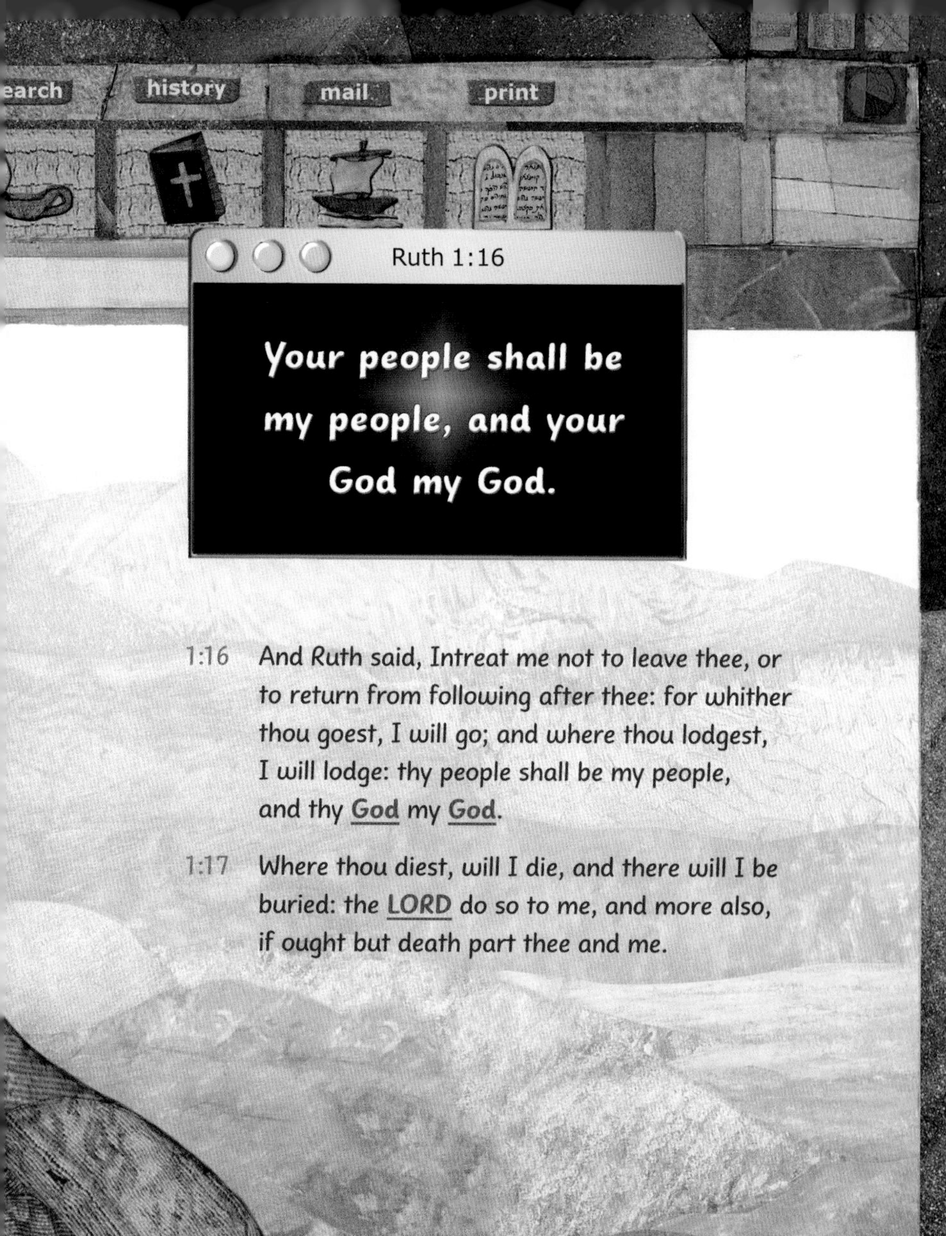
search
history
mail
print
Ruth 1:16
Your people shall be my people, and your God my God.

1:16 And Ruth said, Intreat me not to leave thee, or
to return from following after thee: for whither
thou goest, I will go; and where thou lodgest,
I will lodge: thy people shall be my people,
and thy God my God.

1:17 Where thou diest, will I die, and there will I be
buried: the LORD do so to me, and more also,
if ought but death part thee and me.

1:18 When she saw that she was stedfastly minded to go with her, then she left speaking unto her.

1:19 So they two went until they came to Bethlehem. And it came to pass, when they were come to Bethlehem, that all the city was moved about them, and they said, Is this Naomi?

1:20 And she said unto them, Call me not Naomi, call me Mara: for the Almighty hath dealt very **bitterly** with me.

1:21 I went out full and the LORD hath brought me home again empty: why then call ye me Naomi, seeing the LORD hath testified against me, and the Almighty hath **afflicted** me?

1:22 So Naomi returned, and Ruth the Moabitess, her daughter in law, with her, which returned out of the country of Moab: and they came to Bethlehem in the beginning of barley harvest.

2:1 And Naomi had a kinsman of her husband's, a mighty man of wealth, of the family of Elimelech; and his name was Boaz.

2:2 And Ruth the Moabitess said unto Naomi, Let me now go to the field, and glean ears of corn after him in whose sight I shall find grace. And she said unto her, Go, my daughter.

2:3 And she went, and came, and gleaned in the field after the reapers: and her hap was to light on a part of the field belonging unto Boaz, who was of the kindred of Elimelech.

2:4 And, behold, Boaz came from Bethlehem, and said unto
the reapers, **The LORD be with you**. And they answered
him, **The LORD bless thee**.

2:5 Then said Boaz unto his servant that was set over the
reapers, Whose damsel is this?

2:6 And the servant that was set over the reapers answered
and said, It is the Moabitish damsel that came back with
Naomi out of the country of Moab:

2:7 And she said, I pray you, let me glean and gather after
the reapers among the sheaves: so she came, and hath
continued even from the morning until now, that she
tarried a little in the house.

2:8 Then said Boaz unto Ruth, Hearest thou not, my daughter?
Go not to glean in another field, neither go from hence, but
abide here fast by my maidens:

2:9 Let thine eyes be on the field that they do reap, and go
thou after them: have I not charged the young men that
they shall not touch thee? and when thou art athirst, go
unto the vessels, and drink of that which the young men
have drawn.

2:10 Then she fell on her face, and bowed herself to the ground,
and said unto him, Why have I found grace in thine eyes,
that thou shouldest take knowledge of me, seeing I am a
stranger?

2:11 And Boaz answered and said unto her, It hath fully been shewed me, all that thou hast done unto thy mother in law since the death of thine husband: and how thou hast left thy father and thy mother, and the land of thy nativity, and art come unto a people which thou knewest not heretofore.

2:12 The LORD recompense thy work, and a full reward be given thee of the LORD God of Israel, under whose wings thou art come to trust.

2:13 Then she said, Let me find favour in thy sight, my lord; for that thou hast **comforted** me, and for that thou hast spoken **friendly** unto thine handmaid, though I be not like unto one of thine handmaidens.

2:14 And Boaz said unto her, At mealtime come thou hither, and eat of the bread, and dip thy morsel in the vinegar. And she sat beside the reapers: and he reached her parched corn, and she did eat, and was sufficed, and left.

2:15 And when she was risen up to glean, Boaz commanded his young men, saying, Let her glean even among the sheaves, and reproach her not:

2:16 And let fall also some of the handfuls of purpose for her, and leave them, that she may glean them, and rebuke her not.

2:17 So she gleaned in the field until even, and beat out that she had gleaned: and it was about an ephah of barley.

2:18 And she took it up, and went into the city: and her mother in law saw what she had gleaned: and she brought forth, and gave to her that she had reserved after she was sufficed.

2:19 And her mother in law said unto her, Where hast thou gleaned to day? and where wroughtest thou? blessed be he that did take knowledge of thee. And she shewed her mother in law with whom she had wrought, and said, The man's name with whom I wrought to day is Boaz.

2:20 And Naomi said unto her daughter in law, Blessed be he of the LORD, who hath not left off his **kindness** to the living and to the dead. And Naomi said unto her, The man is near of kin unto us, one of our next kinsmen.

2:21 And Ruth the Moabitess said, He said unto me also, Thou shalt keep fast by my young men, until they have ended all my harvest.

2:22 And Naomi said unto Ruth her daughter in law, It is good, my daughter, that thou go out with his maidens, that they meet thee not in any other field.

2:23 So she kept fast by the maidens of Boaz to glean unto the end of barley harvest and of wheat harvest; and dwelt with her mother in law.

3:1 Then Naomi her mother in law said unto her, My daughter, shall I not seek rest for thee, that it may be well with thee?

3:2 And now is not Boaz of our kindred, with whose maidens thou wast? Behold, he winnoweth barley to night in the threshingfloor.

3:3 Wash thyself therefore, and anoint thee, and put thy raiment upon thee, and get thee down to the floor: but make not thyself known unto the man, until he shall have done eating and drinking.

3:4 And it shall be, when he lieth down, that thou shalt mark the place where he shall lie, and thou shalt go in, and uncover his feet, and lay thee down; and he will tell thee what thou shalt do.

3:5 And she said unto her, All that thou sayest unto me I will do.

3:6 And she went down unto the floor, and did according to all that her mother in law bade her.

3:7 And when Boaz had eaten and drunk, and his heart was merry, he went to lie down at the end of the heap of corn: and she came softly, and uncovered his feet, and laid her down.

3:8 And it came to pass at midnight, that the man was afraid, and turned himself: and, behold, a woman lay at his feet.

3:9 And he said, Who art thou? And she answered, I am Ruth thine handmaid: spread therefore thy skirt over thine handmaid; for thou art a near kinsman.

3:10 And he said, Blessed be thou of the **LORD**, my daughter: for thou hast shewed more **kindness** in the latter end than at the beginning, inasmuch as thou followedst not young men, whether poor or rich.

3:11 And now, my daughter, fear not; I will do to thee all that thou requirest: for all the city of my people doth know that thou art a **virtuous** woman.

3:12 And now it is true that I am thy near kinsman: howbeit there is a kinsman nearer than I.

3:13 Tarry this night, and it shall be in the morning, that if he will perform unto thee the part of a kinsman, well; let him do the kinsman's part: but if he will not do the part of a kinsman to thee, then will I do the part of a kinsman to thee, as the LORD liveth: lie down until the morning.

3:14 And she lay at his feet until the morning: and she rose up before one could know another. And he said, Let it not be known that a woman came into the floor.

3:15 Also he said, Bring the vail that thou hast upon thee, and hold it. And when she held it, he measured six measures of barley, and laid it on her: and she went into the city.

3:16 And when she came to her mother in law, she said, Who art thou, my daughter? And she told her all that the man had done to her.

3:17 And she said, These six measures of barley gave he me; for he said to me, Go not empty unto thy mother in law.

3:18 Then said she, Sit still, my daughter, until thou know how the matter will fall: for the man will not be in rest, until he have finished the thing this day.

4:1 Then went Boaz up to the gate, and sat him down there: and, behold, the kinsman of whom Boaz spake came by; unto whom he said, Ho, such a one! turn aside, sit down here. And he turned aside, and sat down.

4:2 And he took ten men of the elders of the city, and said, Sit ye down here. And they sat down.

4:3 And he said unto the kinsman, Naomi, that is come again out of the country of Moab, selleth a parcel of land, which was our brother Elimelech's:

4:4 And I thought to advertise thee, saying, Buy it before the inhabitants, and before the elders of my people. If thou wilt redeem it, **redeem** it: but if thou wilt not **redeem** it, then tell me, that I may know: for there is none to **redeem** it beside thee; and I am after thee. And he said, I will **redeem** it.

4:5 Then said Boaz, What day thou buyest the field of the hand of Naomi, thou must buy it also of Ruth the Moabitess, the wife of the dead, to **raise up** the name of the dead upon his inheritance.

4:6 And the kinsman said, I cannot **redeem** it for myself, lest I mar mine own inheritance: **redeem** thou my right to thyself; for I cannot **redeem** it.

4:7 Now this was the manner in former time in Israel concerning redeeming and concerning changing, for to confirm all things; a man plucked off his shoe, and gave it to his neighbour: and this was a testimony in Israel.

4:8 Therefore the kinsman said unto Boaz, Buy it for thee. So he drew off his shoe.

4:9 And Boaz said unto the elders, and unto all the people, Ye are witnesses this day, that I have bought all that was Elimelech's, and all that was Chilion's and Mahlon's, of the hand of Naomi.

4:10 Moreover Ruth the Moabitess, the wife of Mahlon, have I purchased to be my wife, to raise up the name of the dead upon his inheritance, that the name of the dead be not cut off from among his brethren, and from the gate of his place: ye are witnesses this day.

4:11 And all the people that were in the gate, and the elders, said, We are witnesses. The LORD make the woman that is come into thine house like Rachel and like Leah, which two did build the house of Israel: and do thou worthily in Ephratah, and be famous in Bethlehem:

4:12 And let thy house be like the house of Pharez, whom Tamar bare unto Judah, of the seed which the LORD shall give thee of this young woman.

4:13 So Boaz took Ruth, and she was his wife: and when he went in unto her, the LORD gave her conception, and she bare a son.

4:14 And the women said unto Naomi, Blessed be the LORD, which hath not left thee this day without a kinsman, that his name may be famous in Israel.

4:15 And he shall be unto thee **a restorer of thy life**, and a **nourisher** of thine old age: for thy daughter in law, which **love**th thee, which is better to thee than seven sons, hath born him.

4:16 And Naomi took the child, and laid it in her bosom, and became nurse unto it.

4:17 And the women her neighbours gave it a name, saying, There is a son born to Naomi; and they called his name Obed: he is the father of Jesse, the father of David.

4:18 Now these are the generations of Pharez: Pharez begat Hezron,

4:19 And Hezron begat Ram, and Ram begat Amminadab,

4:20 And Amminadab begat Nahshon, and Nahshon begat Salmon,

4:21 And Salmon begat Boaz, and Boaz begat Obed,

4:22 And Obed begat Jesse, and Jesse begat David.

1:6 And Jesse begat David the king; and David the king begat Solomon of her that had been the wife of Urias;

1:7 And Solomon begat Roboam; and Roboam begat Abia; and Abia begat Asa;

1:8 And Asa begat Josaphat; and Josaphat begat Joram; and Joram begat Ozias;

1:9 And Ozias begat Joatham; and Joatham begat Achaz; and Achaz begat Ezekias;

1:10 And Ezekias begat Manasses; and Manasses begat Amon; and Amon begat Josias;

1:11 And Josias begat Jechonias and his brethren, about the time they were carried away to Babylon:

1:12 And after they were brought to Babylon, Jechonias begat Salathiel; and Salathiel begat Zorobabel;

1:13 And Zorobabel begat Abiud; and Abiud begat Eliakim; and Eliakim begat Azor;

1:14 And Azor begat Sadoc; and Sadoc begat Achim; and Achim begat Eliud;

1:15 And Eliud begat Eleazar; and Eleazar begat Matthan; and Matthan begat Jacob;

1:16 And Jacob begat Joseph the husband of Mary, of whom was born Jesus, who is called

Matthew

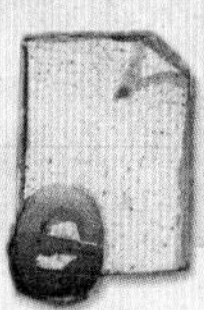

Ruth

Testimony
for
Christ

Testimony

turn to enter

1. Born Again

"Let the beauty of the Lord our God be upon us."
Psalm 90:16

Easter Sunday, April 2004. I had queried every one of the agents belonging to the venerable Association of Author Representatives (AAR) and was staring at a dismally fat pile of over 600 rejection letters for my first book, *Goodbye Gutenberg.* I had also queried most major and midsized New York publishers, many two or three times. "A glorious Renaissance is coming," I proclaimed. "Books will once again be as beautiful as they were in the Middle Ages." I must have spent a thousand dollars on postage and another five hundred on telephone calls. Just about all of them ignored me. A few laughed at me. A few even mocked me. My eyes watered, and I began to weep.

To get my mind off things, I asked my husband to help me organize some of our bookshelves. He showed me a beautiful little volume called the *Illuminated Gospels*. I had neglected it earlier because it's not really "illuminated" in the traditional sense. The body copy is set in a black Roman serif font on a white background. But it does have some lovely color paintings from the Middle Ages and a sensuous velvet blue cloth cover. Seeing the distress in my eyes, my husband held my hand and began to read from the book of Matthew. He read several pages from the Sermon on the Mount and then came upon this verse: "If you have faith as a grain of mustard seed, you will tell this mountain, Move from here to there, and it will move; and nothing will be impossible for you" (Matthew 17:20).

Suddenly my eyes widened, my pupils dilated, my heart pounded. I felt the indescribable awe and excitement of discovering the words of the Lord for the first time, even though for years I had taught the Bible as "literature" in secular classrooms. Passages I had read dozens, maybe even hundreds of times, I now understood for the first time. What was once hidden was then revealed. I was one of the lost sheep of the house of Israel, but now I understood the meaning of the word Gospel, of Good News. Christ came into my heart at that moment. I was born again. My life would never be the same.

I no longer see the Gospels as "literature." I see them as Truth with a capital T. Christ filled a vacuum in my life, in a way that no other book or religion has ever done. It finally occurred to me: birth is not destiny. If your mother is Jewish, you are taught to believe that you are Jewish. One has "Jewish blood." Most Jews don't choose to be Jews; they are born Jewish and told they are Jewish. And this explains, at least in my case, why it never occurred to me that I could be anything else.

But Christianity is a religion of choice. To be a Christian is to be born again. And on that Easter Sunday, while listening to my husband read from the book of Matthew, I was born again.

During the next few months, my husband and I sat hand in hand, reading nightly from the Gospels. We read again from Matthew, about how Peter and Andrew became fishers of men. We discovered in 1 Corinthians 7:7 that each of us has a special gift; and in 1 John 2:27 that there is something each of us is uniquely called to do. Right then we knew: we were called to present the Gospels in a beautiful new way, starting with the book of Matthew. We would put our worldly plans aside, borrow heavily from our credit cards, and trust in the Lord. We would stand up and be counted as two young ambassadors for Christ, called to spark a Renaissance of beautiful Bibles.

2. A Renaissance Whose Time Has Come

"Blessed is he that readeth." Revelation 1:3

Permit me to share with you an astonishing fact. It is so astonishing that at first you may not believe me. But if you search in hundreds of bookstores and spend hundreds of hours searching the Internet, reading trade journals and studying the lists of religious publishers, as I have, you will not find a single Bible - for adults - which has modern, full color illuminations of scenes from the Gospels. I recently discovered one magnificent exception (*The St. John's Bible*, which I will discuss later), but otherwise you will not find a contemporary Bible with such scenes as *Madonna and Child, The Calming of the Storm, The Sermon on the Mount, The Temptation, The Calling of the Disciples, The Triumphal Entry,* or *the Crucifixion.* Not a single one.

Whenever I share this astonishing fact - especially with writers and those interested in the publishing business - they invariably say, "Oh no, that can't be. I'm sure if you do a Google search you'll find lots of illuminated Bibles." And so I have. There is not a single one.

I recently examined every one of the 217 different Bibles for sale at my local Barnes and Noble. 206 were printed in black and white; nine used a second color, and only two used more than two colors in the body copy. On the Internet, I found a few children's Bibles in color, such as the *DK Illustrated Family Bible*; five black and white Bibles with a separate section of color photographs or paintings, such as those of Thomas Kinkade; and a few obscure devotionals and works of calligraphy with selections from the Bible in color. But for adults, I could not find a single complete Bible, or even a single complete New Testament, or even a single complete book of the Gospels with a contemporary rendition of the life and teachings of Jesus Christ. Not a single one.

In a broad survey of the state of religious publishing, a recent *Publishers Weekly* cover story concluded, "There is no Artists Bible (yet)." (October 11, 2004). We can boast of many marvels in this year of our Lord, 2005, but a fully illuminated Bible, created by a contemporary artist or designer, is not one of them.

Every year I meet people who make a New Year's resolution to read the Bible cover to cover. And every year, it seems, so many people who make this resolution fall short. Do we blame them? How many of us have the stamina to stare at 66 books and more than a thousand pages of small black type? Xerox recently compiled the results of several reputable studies showing that, if properly designed, color visuals can increase our willingness to read by up to 80%; retention by up to 60%; and comprehension up to 70%. Imagine how many more people might read the Bible if it was beautifully designed in color!

Thomas Nelson Publishers recently asked hundreds of teenage girls why they don't read the Bible. The number one reason? Because it's "freaky looking." In a thousand pages, a million words, no one could have said it better. Leave it to teenage girls to sum up the whole issue in two simple words. Modern black and white books - including the Bible - are "freaky looking." The teenage girls said they like to read magazines, so Nelson set out to redesign the Bible into a magazine format. What a concept!

Revolve: The Complete New Testament sold several hundred thousand copies in its first year and was the hottest selling Bible for teens in America. Nelson then published *Refuel: The Complete New Testamen*t for teenage boys, in a similar format, showing a hip adolescent strumming his guitar on the cover. The cover screams one word: cool! The design firm of *Revolve* is the same firm that designed posters and music jackets for U2 and Harley Davidson. Other publishers have jumped on the bandwagon with their own full color magazine Bibles for teens, which sell for under $20.

Many parents and pastors have lauded the intent, but complained that the magazine format, by intermingling Biblical text with beauty tips, pop culture quizzes and adolescent preoccupations, demeans the message. The words of our Lord are presented in a small black font on a white background, while the fashion tips scream loudly in bold colors and bold fonts. Parents worry that their children may be distracted by all the colorful sidebars and overlook the small black and white words of the Bible itself.

Fortunately, the magazine format is just one of a thousand possible ways of presenting the Gospels. I believe that the majority of Christian readers would prefer that the words of Jesus be the largest, the boldest, and the most beautiful; that the artwork and designs be the deepest expressions of piety and faith; and that each page be infused with the Holy Spirit.

Jesus admonishes us not to put new wine into old bottles, lest the bottles burst (Matthew 9:17). The Gospels are eternally new wine, but the bottle we now put them in, the old black and white format, has been rendered obsolete by our visual age (pages 46-47). The resounding success of the magazine format is evidence that a new generation is screaming for new Bibles in new kinds of bottles - new colors, new designs, new visual ways of expressing their faith in the Lord.

If millions of teens are reading magazine format Bibles today, in what formats will they read the Bible in their 20s and 30s? They will *never* - and I mean *never* - return to the old black and white format. Not willingly, at least. Black and white text is blasphemy to their eyes, sacrilege to their visual values. As they get older, they will desire more spiritually satisfying formats.

"Blessed are your eyes." Matthew 13:16

We are taught to "outgrow" our childhood books. We are taught that reading small black print is a sign of "maturity," a "progression" into adulthood. Yet we are born into a world of color. Everything we see, touch and discover is in color. Our first experiences with letters and words are often in color. Then one day, around the age of six or seven, we are thrust into an artificial universe of black text crammed into a box and printed on dull white paper. Is this progress? In this colorful age of multimedia, why should we ask our children - and even ourselves - to stare at hundreds of pages of black text? Why do we adults no longer prize beauty in the written word?

The John Newbery Medal is awarded each year for the most distinguished contribution to American literature for children. The Caldecott Medal is awarded each year for the best American picture book for children. There are no design prizes of similar stature for adults. Is beauty just for kids?

"Except ye be converted, and become as little children, ye shall not enter into the kingdom of heaven," we read in Matthew 18:3. Christ is asking us to see the world differently, to become newborn spiritual children. Now we can become newborn spiritual readers, too. Now we can read and see like children, with visual innocence and visual joy.

3. The Church's Love Affair with Beautiful Books

"In the Middle Ages, beauty was taken to be the visible expression of truth." Natasa Golob

The codex book was a key technology in the early spread of Christianity. Rather than struggle with lengthy scrolls, evangelists could quickly flip through the Bible, find key passages, and apply them to a given situation. But art historians such as J.J.G. Alexander, Kurt Weitzmann and Christopher de Hamel have demonstrated that the colorful illumination of these books also played a key role in helping Christianity attract a large audience. The medieval monk and scholar Bede tells us that St. Augustine of Canterbury, traveling to Ireland in 597 A.D., was scheduled to meet with King Ethelberht of Kent. As he walked across the meadow toward the King, he held up a cross and a painted image of Christ. Such imagery - and the marriage of such imagery to the written word - had an enormous impact on audiences around the world.

Evangelists used colorful imagery to convert an illiterate population to Christianity, but they also wanted books of great beauty for themselves. Aristocrats, dukes, monks, priests and princes shared a burning desire for beautiful books. Gerald of Wales, who visited Ireland and poured over the *Book of Kells*, famously remarked, "The more often I see the book, the more carefully I study it, the more I am lost in ever-fresh Amazement, and I see more wonders in the book. Look closely and you will penetrate the very shrine of art. You will see intricacies so delicate and so subtle, with colors so fresh and vivid, that you might say all this was the work of an angel and not of a man."

When was the last time any of us had such an experience, felt this way about a book? A book of words, deep meaningful words? Even today, more than a thousand years after its creation, people come from all over the world to see the *Book of Kells*. Street signs point visitors to the library at Trinity College, Dublin. There is an ever present circle of astonished visitors huddled around the sacred pages. The gorgeous decorated letters have an uncanny ability to attract audiences. Even nonbelievers marveled - and still marvel - at the beautiful adornment of God's Word.

"The great Church festivals such as Christmas and Easter were always written in red ink and from this we get the phrase red letter days," writes the scholar Charles Goodrum. "Lesser festivals and saints' days were in black, and anniversaries of the local saints and churches were inscribed in blue." Brown was the most popular color. In fact, a large number - maybe even most - of the books and Bibles from late antiquity and the Middle Ages were written in brown. The oldest surviving complete New Testament, the *Codex Vaticanus*, was written in brown, while the *Codex Sinaiticus*, also among the oldest, was written in brown and red. The *Book of Kells* was likewise written in brown; scribes saved their black carbon ink for special occasions such as the carpet pages, where black made a powerful impact with the contrasting reds, purples and yellows.

A famous decree among the Cistercians of the 12th century banned the use of gold and historiated initials in books. "Letters should be of one color and not painted," it proclaimed. Scholars have interpreted this as "an expression of ascetic self-denial." The Cistercian tradition is especially poignant because, despite the decree, the Cistercians are well known for their colorful illuminations of books. Many scribes interpreted the decree as license to create silhouetted letters of great beauty, which they then colored by pen in red, blue or green inks. As long as the letters were still legible as capitals or uncials, many scribes believed that they were not violating the decree. Still other scribes ignored the decree entirely, so intense was their desire for beauty.

The great Cistercian St. Bernard instructed his scribes, "Do not allow yourself to be ignorant of beauty, if you do not wish to be in company with ugliness." Bernard cherished his personal Bible, which he had decorated with gold letters, colorful grotesques and wild animals. "Beauty is the most wonderful lily," he said. "Its charm and image are the essence of God."

Short attention spans, it is often remarked, are a "symptom" of the media saturated age we live in. The illuminated manuscripts of medieval Europe suggest otherwise. *The Moralized Bible*, for instance, "required commentary texts that were short, to the point, easily understood, and conveniently illustrated," explains the scholar Gerald Guest. The desire for information that is short, to the point, easily understood, and conveniently illustrated may be universal across times and cultures. It is by no means symptomatic of our age. *The Moralized Bible*, with its gold circular frames, colorful initials, clean illustrations, and rhythmic interplay between word and image is one of the great illuminated manuscripts of the 13th century. As we flip through the pages and our eyes move up and down and back and forth, we experience a kind of animation in our minds. We see the medieval mind at work, a mind that, the more I study it, has much in common with our own.

Gilded manuscripts such as *The Moralized Bible* were no mere lavish indulgence; they were symbols of the celestial kingdom and the splendor of God's word. In the 8th century, Saint Boniface asked that the Scriptures be written in gold letters so that the words "may shine in gold to the glory of the Father in Heaven." Abbot Suger of St. Denis marveled at how gold "carries his mind from the material to the spiritual world." And a scribe of Charlemagne's court wrote that gilded letters "promise golden kingdoms and a lasting good without end."

The spiritual resonance of ornament and decoration, their potential to add a deeper dimension to our books and Bibles, has been entirely lost to us. As Richard of Saint Victor said, to see the spiritual in a decorated letter is to see "with the eyes of the dove." And as the Armenian Saint Nerses Shnorhali said, the illumination of God's word helps us "to understand what the spiritual pleasures and imperishable beauties are."

"I am the light of the world," said Christ (John 8:12). The medieval scribes could think of no better way to express their reverence for this metaphor of profound beauty than to write in the colors of light, most often gold and silver on a black or ruby red background. In the sixth century, Pope Gregory the Great avidly collected colorful manuscripts, one called the *Pastoral Rule*, which used green, yellow and purpura colored text. The Church had a thousand year love affair with beautiful Bibles - until Gutenberg.

4. Gutenberg And The End Of Beauty

"The most visible difference between any manuscript of the Middle Ages and later printed books is that the majority of manuscripts are in more than one color. Even the most humble of medieval books include headings in red and initials perhaps in red and blue. Many are dazzlingly polychrome or filled with gold. Most printed books, even now, are black and white. Color was a casualty of printing."

Christopher de Hamel,
author of The Book: A History of the Bible

"In the 5,000 years since the development of writing, readers have been reduced to staring at letters of identical size and color, arranged in lines of identical length, on pages of identical size and color. Readers, in a sense, are no longer asked to see; they are simply asked to interpret the code."

Mitchell Stephens,
author of The Rise of the Image, the Fall of the Word

In my early years as a high school teacher, many people said to me that saying goodbye to the Gutenberg style, black and white Bible was a frivolous dream - at best. One critic even called me "Madame Nobody" for daring to suggest that young people would read more if their books were as attractive as movies and music videos. Yet this book is not an aberration - it *cannot* be an aberration - because it was created on a single Macintosh computer that most any American can afford to own. What you hold in your hands is tangible evidence, solid proof that this Renaissance has already begun.

Pause a moment. Flip through the pages of this book. Is it even thinkable that thousands of other talented young designers and writers will let me have this God given treasure all to myself? That everyone else of my generation will resign themselves to reading and writing in the "freaky looking," old style black and white format, and that when historians look back at the books of our day, only Ruth Rimm designed an adult Bible in such vibrant colors, only Ruth Rimm proclaimed this coming Renaissance? Preposterous!

Frankly, my friends, it is preposterous to think that our new technologies will have no impact on the visual experience of reading our books and Bibles. It is preposterous to think that the coming generations will ignore these exciting new technologies and blindly follow the old visual clichés of their elders when it comes to reading and writing. Preposterous, indeed!

If we could somehow transport the scribes and illuminators of ages past into our own milieu, they would be astonished by our new writing technologies and embrace them wholeheartedly.

One medieval scribe, speaking for many, remarked that his work "dims the sight, bows the spine, cracks the ribs and breaks the aching back." Yet he and countless other scribes persevered because they believed in the value of making their books beautiful.

In the 11th Canto of *Purgatory*, Dante said that the illuminated pages of Franco of Bologna "smile more." In just a few words, Dante brilliantly captured both the triumph and the visual demise of the written word before and after Gutenberg. The printing press is assuredly one of the great inventions of all time. It allowed us to make books quickly and cheaply, fueling an extraordinary hunger for knowledge and information. But books quickly lost that colorful smile of which Dante spoke. Black words, wedged into a rectangle and printed uniformly on dull white paper, soon became the norm. "We increased knowledge after Gutenberg," writes Whodini. "But we also lost, sorrowfully, our ability to see."

Gutenberg invented not only a new way of printing but also a new way of seeing and a new way of thinking. As the scholar Gerald Janecek observed, "Gutenberg's legacy of linear movable type and mass produced books is such an innate part of modern Western culture that we are almost blind to its effects on our thought patterns and cultural assumptions." Gutenberg initially designed his Bibles to look like fine calligraphic manuscripts. He even left room for letters to be colored and decorated by hand. But for technological and economic reasons (certainly not for aesthetic reasons), black text in a rectangle - without color or illustration - soon became the norm. Now, in a media-saturated, richly visual age, when we stare at a page of black text, we often experience blackout - literally. What is important? Where to begin? Consider the irony that in Gutenberg's day, printing was known as a "schwarze Kunst," a black art. We think the Dark Ages are behind us when, in fact, they are right in front of us.

Some educators and technology gurus have mistakenly assumed that if you take black and white text and simply transfer it to the screen, young people are more likely to read it. Yet in my classroom, I find that my students love paper. The debate about the future of reading and writing is not between screen and print. It is between rectangular blocks of black and white text and colorfully designed pages. It is between the Gutenberg cliché and a vernacular that speaks directly to the eyes. It is between the Old Way of Reading and the New.

Publishers Weekly compiled a list of the best-selling book for each year from 1900 to 1999. Almost all of them were designed in the standard black and white format. Compare this to a list of the most popular books created between 1300 and 1399, the century before Gutenberg invented his printing press. The reverse is true: almost all of them were beautifully illuminated in color. Here we are, curators of the most advanced technological culture in history, and our books are among the ugliest of any era.

There is a widespread misconception that the Bible is the all time bestseller. In the Middle Ages, it most definitely was not. The bestsellers were Books of Hours, Devotionals, Psalters, Breviaries and individual selections or volumes of the Bible, such as the *Book of Revelation*. During the Renaissance, readers almost always preferred smaller volumes with less text and more illustrations.

In order to print all 66 books of the Bible in one volume, it is necessary to cram an enormous amount of text onto each page. The early writers of the Bible did not envision it becoming so large that it becomes a burden. Jesus says, "My yoke is easy, my burden is light" (Matthew 11:30). Individual books create an aura of easiness and lightness, and will get read. Even the magazine format Bibles break up the Old and New Testaments.

The advantage of the black and white Bible will always be that you can carry around the entire Bible in one volume. But even though you can carry it, you can't read it in one sitting or on one trip. Maybe on your next vacation you want to read Genesis or Acts or all of the Psalms. Beautifully designed, individual volumes of the Bible allow you to enjoy these books both verbally and visually, and feel the satisfaction of completion.

The calligraphy of most of the illuminated manuscripts of the Middle Ages is what we would call "large print." Yet the font size of so many of our Bibles is small, creating eyestrain and discomfort. The large print Bibles address this concern, but they are even heavier than standard Bibles, and they are still crammed with text. Designing the Bible in individual volumes allows the reader to enjoy God's Word in a larger font without being burdened by a larger book.

The old style, black and white Bibles will always be around for reference and study, but for pleasure – well, I am not so sure. Even the commentaries of the Middle Ages were often as lavishly decorated as the Scriptures themselves. Our individual volumes can likewise contain beautifully designed commentary.

Individual volumes also allow us to target a specific kind of teaching to the needs of a child or friend. For example, give a beautifully designed *Book of Job* to a friend who has suffered a great deal. Give a beautifully designed edition of the letters of Paul to someone facing considerable obstacles. And so on.

As a newborn in Christ, I was astonished to learn that there are very few editions, even in black and white, with just the letters of Paul. I pray that God will grant me the strength and the resources to create a beautifully designed edition of these divine letters. "Having nothing, but having everything, being poor, but enriching others" just devastates me, along with hundreds of other lines in Paul (2 Corinthians 6:10). I have spent many hours gazing at Renaissance illuminations of his letters to the Romans. My brothers and sisters in Christ, how I ache to share with you this vision! During the Renaissance, they not only read Paul, they experienced him visually. They kissed his wisdom, literally, with their eyes.

And then there are the Acts of the Apostles, and James, and Revelation. And the Psalms, and the Proverbs, and the Prophets. Ohhhh! For five hundred years, we have been depriving ourselves of the joys of experiencing God's Word visually! Now, somehow, miraculously, our generation is poised for a Great Revival of beautiful books and Bibles. What have we done, Lord, to be worthy of such a gift, such a blessing?

Wait a minute. Stop. Time out. Why am I writing like this? Here I am, purporting to announce a Renaissance in beautiful books and Bibles, yet making the announcement in the old way, in black and white! How ridiculous! And here we writers are, typing all day in Microsoft Word, confining ourselves to black and white, while all of these remarkable tools stare right at us!

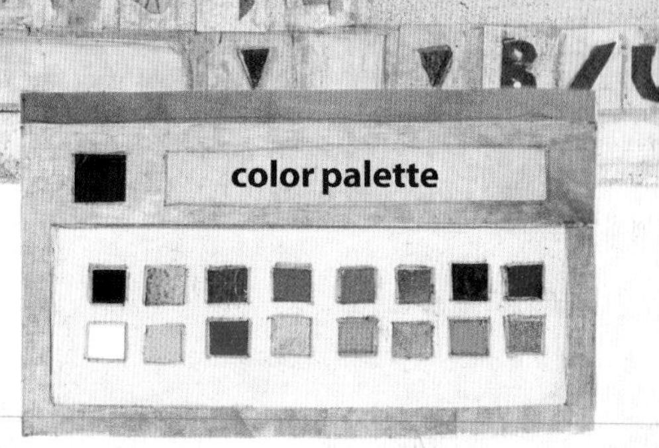

Ah, it is so refreshing, such a relief to be writing in color again! The first thing I will do is change fonts. Before the invention of the printing press, scribes often felt inspired by the Holy Spirit. Their calligraphy often revealed this inspiration to the eyes of the reader. Their words, quite literally, exuded energy and body language that vanished with the advent of print. And so for the Four Gospels I am using a font called Booklady, which was inspired by my own handwriting. (The rebirth of fonts inspired by handwriting is discussed in detail in Goodbye Gutenberg). Next I'm going right for the color palette. Point. Click. Red. Blue. Green. Glory! Halleluyah!

5. Dawn of Designer Bibles

Design is an expression of faith, just as six hundred years ago, decoration was an expression of faith. Design in no way changes the Word of God; rather, it deepens our understanding of it. A beautifully designed Bible invites us to pause before turning the page, to engage in the ancient art of lectio divina, literally "**divine reading**." Through a slow, pious rumination of the text, we are invited to ponder, just as the Virgin Mary "**pondered in her heart**" upon learning that her son was the Christ (**Luke 2:19**).

We no longer use movable type and we no longer make our pages with an olive press. Our presses are digital now. Beautiful Bibles need not be rare, expensive or limited, as they once were, to an elite group of kings, dukes, emperors and aristocrats. With computers, we can do things that no other culture could do. We can visually express our faith in Christ in ways **unimaginable** to previous generations. I hesitate to say "better," but I do believe we have more **opportunities** and **possibilities** than ever before. In the past, they created illuminated Bibles. Now we will create **designer Bibles**.

With our design and color printing technologies getting ever more economical, the dawn of designer Bibles is inevitable. One word: inevitable. It might take another decade or so, but the Gutenberg model has to collapse because it was, in the final analysis, a technological innovation. It was never representative of a universally preferred way of reading and writing. Bring St. Aquinas or St. Bernard back to life, show them a printed black and white Bible, and they would have said that you are crazy to stare at such monotony for hours on end.

Sales of graphic novels are booming, not because they represent the ideal format, but because they are, at the moment, just about the only visual alternative to Gutenberg style novels. Given all we can do with **computers**, they represent only a tiny slice of the possibilities offered by a designer fiction and **designer Bibles** genre. Children today are reared on video games, computers, movies and television, all of which project a much different visual aesthetic. Art Spiegelman, author of the brilliant and influential graphic novel, Maus, recently warned of the "collapse" of this market niche as early as 2007.

My initial sketches for the Gospel of Matthew relied mostly on Old Master paintings of the story of Christ. But I soon realized that we see the world much differently today, and that our art must mirror the **visual soul** of our times. **To set the Gospels in the scenery of your own times is, in fact, the predominant tradition of art.** Brueghel sets the Gospels in 16th century Flanders; El Greco in Toledo; Molenaer in the Netherlands; Cole in the Hudson River Valley, just a few miles from my home. Gaze up at the ceiling of the Sistine Chapel or leaf through any art book

with Christian imagery: you will most often see the visual world - the clothing, the architecture, the weaponry, the symbols - in which the artists, and not Christ, inhabited.

Alejandra worked entirely by **hand**, while I worked entirely by **computer**. My goal has been to marry tradition and technology, to create a Bible that communes with the past yet breathes in the present.

When historians look back at the Bibles Alejandra and I produced, they will recognize instantly when they were created: at the dawn of the **Internet Age**. It is very much a part of my testimony and my faith: that two thousand years later, while standing on the shoulders of science,

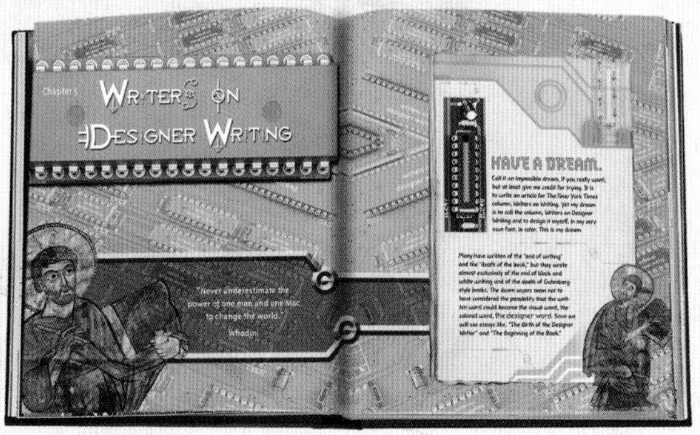

Goodbye Gutenberg, Chapter 5, Writers on Designer Writing. St. Luke is shown on the left, with St. Mark on the right. Both are holding Bibles illuminated in gold. The chapter explores the revival of beautifully designed books and Bibles using new technologies.

we still revere the words of Christ. These pages look very different from anything you will find in any of the illuminated manuscripts of ages past. Yet the message is the same - and this itself is part of the message.

"Jesus Christ the same yesterday, and today, and forever" (Hebrews 13:8). Amen. Our faith in Christ is even stronger today, because we have chosen Christ despite the moral and spiritual bankruptcy that so often pervades our scientific age. In the Middle Ages and Renaissance, the Church had so much power that artists typically had no choice but to paint religious iconography, whether they believed or not. But today

Goodbye Gutenberg, Chapter 5, Writers on Designer Writing.
Christians of Medieval Spain sought to overcome their spiritual crisis through the creation of beautiful Bibles. They are renowned for their magnificent illuminations of the Book of Revelation. Many of their symbols are strikingly similar to computer circuitry.

the creation of faith-based, Christian art is entirely a matter of choice. Alejandra and I were under no pressure to create a designer Bible that adheres to any Church doctrine; if anything, the artworld often rewards the most blasphemous works.

I learned from the Italian painter and monk Fra Angelico never to sit at my computer without first saying a prayer. I ask the Lord to be the shepherd of my eyes. With each mouse click, I stretch forth my hand; with each color, I pray that "**peace and love be multiplied**" through the creation of beautiful Bibles (**Jude 1:2**).

People sometimes ask me why I use a web browser as the central motif for my Bible or why I portrayed Jesus holding a cell phone. Three words: relevant, relevant, relevant. I asked myself a simple question: if Christ came today, and I was asked to design a printed book in the spirit of the age, what would it look like? It most certainly would not look like a comic book or an illuminated manuscript of the Middle Ages. We live in an age that cries for new symbols. The St. John's Bible has a gorgeous portrait of the Apostle Paul standing in front of modern skyscrapers. Clearly, the Catholic theologians who advised on the project sought to integrate visual symbols of modern life into their Bible. St. Augustine wrote of "**beauty ever ancient ever new**" (**Confessions 10:27**). Each generation must decide which of the ancient symbols to beautify, and which to create anew.

To be a fisher of men and women for the Lord in a technological culture must involve the Internet in some way. This is why I chose an Internet motif and called this the .Christ series. The word "net" is ever so apt, as Jesus said, **"The Kingdom of Heaven is like a net" (Matthew 13:47)**. The great lesson of the parable of the Net is that it attracts all kinds of people and activities, both good and evil. We must not allow the evil in the world - in this case, the evil on the **Internet** - to prevent us from glorifying the good. One person complained to me that because there are things like pornography on the Internet, I am "demeaning" Christ by using an Internet motif. But that's like saying that because there are poisonous fish in the sea, we shouldn't fish; or because some books are bad, we should burn them all. Instead of a seine net, we have an internet; instead of plant fiber, optical fiber. Jesus taught us to go forth and fish, and trust that by his grace we will, ultimately, be separated from evil.

Jesus used illustrations from **everyday work life** and told us to bring him with us wherever we go. **"Lo, I am with you always" (Matthew 28:20)**. I added cell phones and personal digital assistants to some spreads because wherever we go these days - whether to the supermarket, work, school, a restaurant, a hotel, a sporting event, etc. - the air is abuzz with the music of our day; it is a symphony of beeping laptops and chirping blackberries.

Medieval scribes adorned their manuscripts with birds and fish and animals not so much for decoration, but to symbolize their **usefulness**. As Linette Martin explains in **Sacred Doorways**, scribes believed that animals were "created to be eaten, ridden, worn, loaded with burdens, or harvested for quills, fleece or leather. Animals were living bundles of usefulness." Likewise, the **web browsers** and gadgets in this book do not decorate, but remind us of their **usefulness** in **serving our Lord**. Portraying Jesus with a cell phone is a way of reminding ourselves that every time we open our mouths, we should speak with a **pure heart**

Chapter 35

The Visual Vernacular

Goodbye Gutenberg, Chapter 35, The Visual Vernacular. The chapter explores a striking parallel between the shift from Latin to vernacular Bibles 500 years ago and the shift occurring today to Bibles in the "visual vernacular." The old style, black and white Bibles are being transformed into full-color "designer Bibles."

(**Matthew 15:1**). Jesus is, quite literally, calling us. Our love for him should emanate from our voices and reveal itself in words of kindness to others. For **"it is not ye that speak, but the Spirit of your Father which speaketh in you" (Matthew 10:20)**. To compartmentalize Christ, to limit him to a Sunday Church visit, to exalt him only when we are so inclined, is to trivialize Christ. But to **bring him into all aspects of our lives** - which is what he asked us to do - is to acknowledge that wherever we are, and whatever we are doing, **Christ is with us**.

Goodbye Gutenberg, Chapter 4, Writing in the Color of the Stars.

Above left is a Renaissance Book of Hours, while above right is a Bible from the 6th century, written in silver ink on a dark red background. By writing in light colors on dark backgrounds, medieval artists and scribes created a deeply spiritual - and visual - reading experience.

A careful examination of the first "Calling of the Disciples" spread on page 52 suggests layers of meaning that may not be obvious at first glance. The large hand holding the cell phone is outside of the browser - in other words, outside of the story. Jesus is inside the story, but his arm holding the cell phone extends toward us. Jesus is both inside and outside, alive in this world, yet not of it. He is literally reaching across time, touching us with his wisdom, and speaking directly to our hearts.

Placing Jesus inside "live" video feeds, in what I call JNN - the Jesus News Network - is likewise a way of emphasizing his presence in an age of instant communication. The video feeds remind us of the immediacy of Christ's message, whereas the artistic web browsers transport us into a world of spirit and imagination. The interplay and contrast between the two mirrors our daily struggle to exalt each moment, to find meaning in the seemingly mundane.

There were numerous possible ways of depicting the Resurrection (page 186). The traditional and obvious way, the literal way, shows an event that happened in the past. But to me, an even greater affirmation of faith is to show the Resurrection as an event unfolding in the present. Jesus looks directly at us from inside a television set and speaks to us "live" from Galilee. Now Christ is risen, and now we can **"teach all nations"** (**Matthew 28:19**) in this glorious age of gadgetry. Notice the printed book on the lower left. I believe that printed books - at the very least, beautifully designed printed books - will continue to hold a hallowed placed in our culture. In fact, one might ultimately credit Christ (and by extension, the great religions of the world) for maintaining a strong literate culture in a multimedia age.

I am also asked about the underlined words throughout the text. Given the Internet motif, they symbolize hyperlinks. Of course, in a printed book such as this, you can't click on them, so I call them hyperwords, or "**hyperlinks to the heart**." Each of us has a treasure chest of **words that link** directly to our hearts. On these pages you can literally see my **love buttons**, and the links that pointed me to Christ.

Christ

I sought a balance between illustration and evocation. The literal illustrations keep us grounded in the reality of the story, while the more evocative designs invite us to feel, to experience the **visual music** of the Christian heart. But just as there are different Churches and different denominations, there are assuredly different ways of presenting his Word. The Apostle Peter wrote of the "**many-colored grace of God**" (**1 *Peter* 4:10**); it is a phrase of striking resonance for our generation. I believe that we will witness the birth of a multiplicity of design

styles. Each designer Bible is a little temple of the living God. And each design style is a testimony of how we visualize our faith in the Lord. A diversity of design styles is a healthy sign; despite our differences, we are one body in Christ. **"Now there are diversities of gifts, but the same Spirit" (1 Corinthians 12:4).**

One of the most difficult decisions I had to make was which translation to use. I sought counsel from many highly regarded people, but no definitive answer emerged. If anything, this Renaissance will be fueled, in part, by the need for designer Bibles in multiple translations and

Goodbye Gutenberg, Chapter 32, Ornament and Decoration. One of the most common misunderstandings of ornament and decoration is that they are "superfluous" and do not add any "meaning" or "substance" to a work. The chapter explores how medieval scribes regarded ornament as an expression of their reverence for God.

multiple design styles. And not only multiple English versions, but also multiple language versions. Several friends from Church would like a French or Spanish or Chinese edition to send to relatives back home. One of the glories of designing Bibles in the computer age is that the same artwork can be easily reformatted into another language. We need only cut and paste, and presto: the same beautiful Bible is now available in another translation. Ultimately, the Bible is true and enduring in all translations. **"The word of the Lord endureth forever" (1 Peter 1:25).**

If we limit beauty to things made entirely by hand, then the commissioning of beautiful Bibles remains an elite enterprise. Only the most affluent will afford them, just as in the past only a Duke of Berry or a King Charles of France could afford them. The St. John's Bible is the culmination of a seven year, multi-million dollar effort. Made mostly by hand, it is a unique and gorgeous artifact, and I recommend the facsimile edition. But new technologies have liberated us from the need for royal patronage or multi-million dollar budgets to create a beautiful Bible. **A home studio, an Internet connection, and the Spirit of the Holy Ghost are all we need.**

I am so thankful that the Lord connected me with Alejandra, one of the angels of my life. Christine de Pisan had her Anastasia, and I am honored to say, I have my

Alejandra. We still have never met, even though **our hearts touch daily**. Alejandra lives in California. We know each other only through the **Internet** and telephone calls. I have **connected** with so many others on the Net who have become dear friends as well. Everyone has a similar story to tell. So designing the Gospels for the Internet age - with an Internet motif - is ever so appropriate. By searching in one of these very browsers I even met my lifetime **soulmate** - my husband. Praise the Lord!

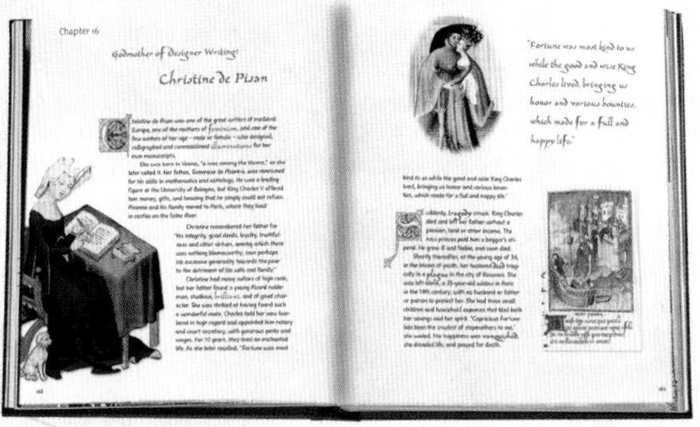

Chapter 16

Godmother of Designer Writing:

Christine de Pisan

"Fortune was most kind to us while the good and wise King Charles lived, bringing us honor and various bounties, which made for a full and happy life."

Goodbye Gutenberg, Chapter 16,
Godmother of Designer Writing: Christine de Pisan.
Pisan was a devout Christian writer who also calligraphed and designed her own books. She wrote her body copy most often in brown and adorned key words and phrases in red, green and blue.

6. Ruth: An Inspiration For All Faiths

Every morning tickles my soul with the realization that my parents named me after Ruth. Shakespeare was wrong: a rose by any other name is still a rose, but a name is a seed that smiles inside the heart. I never noticed it, never knew that quietly sandwiched between my first and last names was my destiny.* The sages tell us that when parents give their child a Jewish name, they are actually experiencing a minor prophecy; for they are Divinely inspired to give the child the name that corresponds to its unique soul.

Only a few pages long, and not very dramatic, the book of **Ruth may be the most important book of our time**. Ruth was a convert, a Gentile, yet the purest of all Jews. She was also the mother of David, Solomon, and Christ; Godmother of the Psalms, the Proverbs, and the Gospels. Miracles sprang from the womb of Ruth, a woman who did for the Jews what no Jewish woman at the time could do.

The lesson of Ruth is simply this: **it matters not what you are born, but what you become.** So I was born a Jew. And you a Christian. And you a Muslim. And you a Buddhist. Why fight over what we were born? The lesson of Ruth is that **religion** is a matter of **Spirit**, not birth.

Ours is a wounded world that cries out for peace. The message of Ruth is that no one tradition can do it alone - especially now, in an age of nuclear

*My maiden name was Valerie Ruth Kirschenbaum

proliferation, terrorism, and biological warfare, when any one tradition has the power to destroy them all. We need thousands of Ruths if we are ever to heal these awful wounds.

For thousands of years, the Gentiles have found comfort and joy in the Jewish stories and Psalms, yet how many Jews have ever read the New Testament, let alone dared to seek comfort in it? I myself could

Goodbye Gutenberg, Chapter 37, Terror in the Arts.
Shown is one of the great images from the Hours of Catherine of Cleves. Medieval and Renaissance illuminators saw beauty as encompassing the entire spectrum of human experience. The chapter draws an analogy between the terrors expressed in religious manuscripts such as this and our own recent experience with 9/11. The creation of visually beautiful books is far more than flower or fluff. Visual books pulsate with the passions, triumphs, and tragedies of the age.

not share in the riches of the Christian message because I was taught that doing so was sacrilege. How astonished I was to learn that Jesus embraced part of the Shema, the daily prayer of Orthodox Jews, in his teaching (**Matthew 22:37**). When asked by his fellow Rabbis which is the most important commandment of all, he combined part of the Shema (**Deuteronomy 6:5**) with a passage from Leviticus (**19:18**). He said **there is nothing greater than to love God and to love each other.**

As a Jew, it was difficult for me to understand what it means to call myself a "sinner." But leave it to Jesus to explain it in terms even a newborn can understand. In the

Goodbye Gutenberg, Chapter 13, Hebrew Illuminated Manuscripts. The chapter explores the Jews' struggle to illuminate their Bibles, despite the Second Commandment prohibition against graven images. The Talmud and other sources tell of Torah scrolls "illuminated in gold."

Greek New Testament, the word for sin is hamartia, originally an archery term which meant "to miss the target." Christ has given us a target of how we should live. And we are sinners because, especially in a world of temptation, we keep missing his divine target, and **"come short of the glory of God"** (**Romans 3:23**).

Another difficult thing for a Jew to understand is what it means to "take up the cross" and follow Jesus. To me, it means the crucifixion of my selfish nature. It means asking the Lord to transform my lowly self into one of the shining lights of the world. It means arising each morning and singing to the Lord, "Take and use me for your glory!" But it also means not becoming proud, or self-righteous, or judgmental. It means recognizing, as Paul taught, that the closer I get to Christ, the more flawed and human I realize I am. I feel so inadequate, so humbled by my inability to share with you how Christ flooded my soul on that Easter Sunday, 2004!

I find so much comfort and joy in having a personal relationship with Christ. But I love and respect those with other views and other experiences of their faith. I do not trouble myself with eschatological questions about who is saved and who is going to Heaven. These are matters for the Lord. A true Christian loves people of all denominations and all faiths. **"Wherein thou judgest another, thou condemnest thyself"** (**Romans 2:1**). To love someone whose beliefs are contrary to your own: is

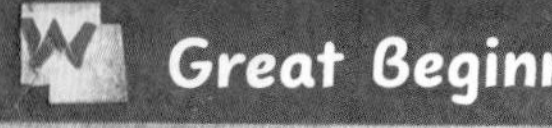

this not what it means to be a true Christian? Of what use is it to love only those like ourselves? **"Him that is weak in the faith receive ye, but not to doubtful disputations" (Romans 14:1).**

Be not scared or offput by those who insist that their way of understanding Christianity must be yours. **"In my father's house are many mansions,"** says Jesus **(John 14:2)**. Salvation is directly through Christ, not your neighbor's flawed interpretation of Christ. As Jesus says, **"By this all will know that you are my disciples, if you have love for one another" (John 13:34).** As Paul says, **"Live peacefully with all men" (Romans 12:18).** And as John says, **"God is love, and he that dwells in love dwells in God" (1 John 4:16).**

Matthew begins with a Genealogy, and I confess that for most of my life I just passed it over, thinking it was dull and of no consequence. But now I understand that the beginning of the book of Matthew is a story of **transformation**, of great beginnings. In that first chapter is one simple word, one simple name that resonates for the ages: Ruth.

There would never have been a Jesse, or a David, or a Solomon, or a Christ, without Ruth - a convert. Thus I have included the book of Ruth, because taken together, if we fast forward from Ruth to Matthew, we can see how **powerful** is the idea of **conversion**. Of what can happen

when one woman makes up her mind to live a Spiritual life and of the impact she can have on the world. Where the Torah teaches us to "**love thy neighbor as thyself,**" (**Leviticus 19:18**), the Hebrew root for neighbor is rea, meaning a friend or, at the very least, someone close to you. But Jesus tells us even to "**love your enemies**" (**Matthew 5:23**). He broadened the definition of rea to include **all people**. From rea came the name Ruth. And from Ruth came a **love** for all.

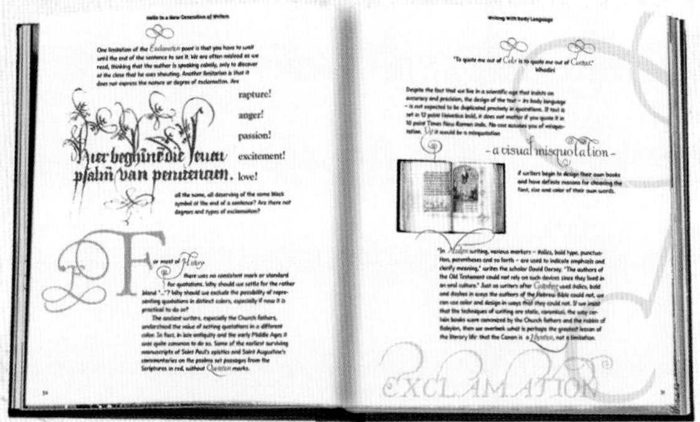

Hello to a New Generation of Writers

One limitation of the Exclamation point is that you have to wait until the end of the sentence to see it. We are often misled as we read, thinking that the author is speaking calmly, only to discover at the close that he was shouting. Another limitation is that it does not express the nature or degree of exclamation. Are

rapture!
anger!
passion!
excitement!
love!

all the same, all deserving of the same black symbol at the end of a sentence? Are there not degrees and types of exclamation?

For most of History there was no consistent mark or standard for quotations. Why should we settle for the rather bland "..."? Why should we exclude the possibility of representing quotations in distinct colors, especially if now it is practical to do so?

The ancient writers, especially the Church fathers, understood the value of setting quotations in a different color. In fact, in late antiquity and the early Middle Ages it was quite common to do so. Some of the earliest surviving manuscripts of Saint Paul's epistles and Saint Augustine's commentaries on the psalms set passages from the Scriptures in red, without Quotation marks.

Writing With Body Language

"To quote me out of Color is to quote me out of Context."
Whodini

Despite the fact that we live in a scientific age that insists on accuracy and precision, the design of the text – its body language – is not expected to be duplicated precisely in quotations. If text is set in 12 point Helvetica bold, it does not matter if you quote it in 10 point Times New Roman italic. No one accuses you of misquotation. Yet it would be a misquotation

– a visual misquotation –

if writers begin to design their own books and have definite reasons for choosing the font, size and color of their own words.

"In Modern writing, various markers – italics, bold type, punctuation, parentheses and so forth – are used to indicate emphasis and clarify meaning," writes the scholar David Dorsey. "The authors of the Old Testament could not rely on such devices since they lived in an oral culture." Just as writers after Gutenberg used italics, bold and dashes in ways the authors of the Hebrew Bible could not, we can use color and design in ways that they could not. If we insist that the techniques of writing are static, canonical, the way certain books were canonized by the Church fathers and the rabbis of Babylon, then we overlook what is perhaps the greatest lesson of the literary life: that the Canon is a Horizon, not a limitation.

EXCLAMATION

Goodbye Gutenberg, Chapter 3, Writing With Body Lanugage. Studies have found that as little as seven percent of human communiation is verbal; most is through sound and body language. This chapter explores how medieval scribes saw calligraphy as a way of imbuing their words with "body language." Today, we can acheive similar results with the thousands of fonts now available to us.

"I come not to deny, but to fulfill," said Jesus (Matthew 5:17). If you are born Jewish and accept Christ into your heart, it does not mean that you deny your heritage. One of the greatest moments of my thirties was when I realized I could be **Jewish** and still **love Christ**, that I could truly call the Hebrew Scriptures and the New Testament by one word - the Bible.

Goodbye Gutenberg, Chapter 7, The Gutenberg Cliché. This chapter traces how books and Bibles changed their appearance before, during and after Gutenberg. The printing press put the grand tradition of beautiful, full color books to sleep; but after 550 years, we are poised for a Great Revival.

7. Neglect Not The Gifts Within Thee

Hundreds of agents and publishers have dismissed this vision of **designer books** and **designer Bibles** as "too revolutionary" or "too far ahead of its time." But when is the time? As Rabbi Hillel asked, "If not now, when? If not us, who?" We live in an age of unprecedented visual stimulation, yet how much of this stimulation is in the service of our Lord? In writing about the future of Christian art, Michael Quenot senses, even in the secular world, "an emerging desire for a different image, one that might serve as the means for mankind's awakening, as a source of fulfillment and peace."

I thank God everyday for humbling me, for sending the obstacles that have tested and fortified my **faith**. I know that somehow, miraculously, the Lord has entered my life to create a **lasting testament to his grace**. And I know that in the next ten years, he will enter the lives of thousands of other artists and designers who, likewise, will create lasting testaments to his grace. Not fads that get new facelifts every year, but **timeless expressions** of piety and **faith**. Let us not design our Bibles merely for the moment, for the Bible is not a momentary book. The Bible is a book for all moments.

I have not a dollar to my name, but I am a millionaire - a millionaire in love, a millionaire in my **faith** in the Lord!

I have nothing, yet I have everything (**2 Corinthians 6:10**). How grateful I am, and how blessed that despite all the obstacles, the Lord has brought us together. You hold in your hands the first fruits of his love for me, as I finish this book on my first birthday as a Christian. Please go to a "real" web browser, and send me an email. Share with me your love.

I know I am lowly. I know there are others far more talented and far more knowledgeable than I, and that they will soon rise up and bless the world with the beauty it deserves. I do not understand why I was called to design the Gospels. If you were to travel the four corners of the earth to gather a list of qualified applicants, I would not have even made the list, let alone have been selected. But Christ did say that even the least among us can do amazing things (**John 14:12**). Christ did say that faith can move mountains (**Matthew 17:20**). A humble soul cannot do it alone, but the book in your hands is proof that with God all things are possible (**Matthew 19:26**).

In these pages you may confront the ecstasy of a newborn in Christ, but please forgive me for any errors or omissions you may see here. I came to the Lord through his Word (in particular, through beautiful illuminations of his Word). I am blessedly ignorant of doctrine. After discussing my design sketches with pastors from various denominations, I hungered for more knowledge and immersed myself in the commentaries of Chambers,

Spurgeon, and Barclay, among others. Then I studied how Rubens, Raphael, Giotto, Tintoretto and dozens of other great artists interpreted the Gospels. But these commentaries soon stifled the **treasures** of my **imagination**; my designs grew sterile, and I lost touch with the Holy Spirit. I stopped reading, stopped studying the doctrines, stopped worrying about whether my designs made me a Baptist or a Catholic or a Universalist. And as quickly as I had lost it, I found it; I was flush with creativity, and knew that the **Spirit of the living God** was with me once more. I was called to design the Gospels not from the head, but from the **heart**.

Goodbye Gutenberg, Chapter 21, Color in Education, Advertising and the Arts. This chapter explores how educators, theologians, monks, artists, and advertisers have each used color to emphasize key words and concepts. Legal decisions, Papal decrees, and theological disputes each had a distinct color scheme and style of illumination.

Jesus is such a **joy** to have in my heart. Yet when I share my testimony with nonreligious or even Catholic friends, they often tell me that the phrase "**born again**" has negative connotations in our culture and that I should "avoid the phrase at all costs." How it pains me to hear that one of the most **beautiful** things we can experience is tarnished by the behavior of the vocal few who misuse it. In Greek, the phrase is gennatha anothen, and it has a double meaning. The King James version always translates it as "born again," but the New International Version translates it as "born from above" and the American Standard Version translates it as "born anew." Have you

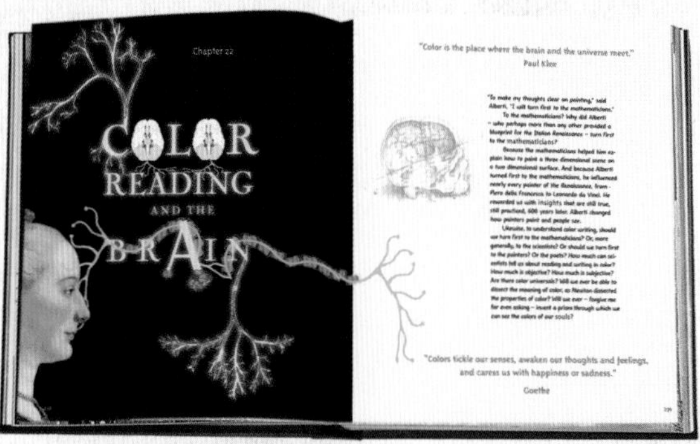

Goodbye Gutenberg, Chapter 22, Color, *Reading* and the Brain. **Recent neuroscientific research has demonstrated that colorfully designed prose stimulates more brain cells and more more regions of the brain than standard black and white text.**

ever arisen one morning desperate for a fresh start? Have you not ever had so many problems, heartbreaks and anxieties that you cried out for help, hoping that someone or something would save you? Or have you ever wished that the past would just wither away, stop haunting you, stop soiling any beauty you might experience in the present moment?

Along comes Jesus, who allows himself to be crucified so that we can be "born anew," **liberated** from our past and **granted a glorious new beginning**. We can find a **new joy**, a **new peace**, a **new love** for our brothers and sisters, a new compassion even for those who dislike us. No one with an open mind and heart can read of the story of Christ without feeling awe - or even, in the words of Paul, **"fear and trembling" (Philippians 2:12)**. The very thought that Jesus gave his life for me, so that I can be free from the tyranny of my own sinful nature, and touch with my heart the very rapture of the heavens, seems so surreal, so unfathomable to me.

Please, my friends, don't judge religion by those who profess to be religious. "**Beware of false prophets**" (**Matthew 7:15**) and of those in America today who supposedly act in Christ's name, deceiving many (**Matthew 24:4**). Read the actual words and teachings of Christ. **"When he was reviled, he did not revile in return; when he suffered, he did not threaten; but he trusted to him who judges justly" (1 Peter 2:21).** Let your heart thaw to the emotional depth and pathos of the Christian message.

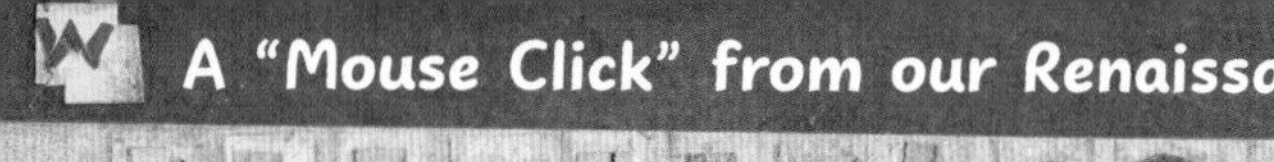

What better fragrance is there than **forgiveness**? What better salt than **compassion**? What better music than **love**?

"Neglect not the gift that is in thee," we read in 1 Timothy 4:14. These words resonate especially for our generation. We really do have the gifts to launch another **Renaissance**. And we have an obligation to do so. To

Dauids complaint. Pfalmes. 239

The Geneva Bible, 1590

He prophesieth of Christ 831 PSALMS 22

oven in the time of thine anger: the LORD shall swallow them up in his wrath, and the fire shall devour them. Mal 4:1

10 Their fruit shalt thou destroy from the earth, and their seed from among the children of men.

11 For they intended evil against thee: they imagined a mischievous device, *which* they are not able *to perform*. Ps 2:1-3

12 Therefore shalt thou make them turn their back, *when* thou shalt make ready *thine arrows* upon thy strings against the face of them. Ps 7:12-13

13 Be thou exalted, LORD, in thine own strength: *so* will we sing and praise thy power. Ps 81:1

PSALM 22

To the chief Musician upon Aijeleth Shahar, A Psalm of David.

MY God, my God, why hast thou forsaken me? *why art thou so* far from helping me, *and from* the words of my roaring?

2 O my God, I cry in the daytime, but thou hearest not; and in the night season, and am not silent.

3 But thou *art* holy, *O thou* that inhabitest the praises of Israel.

4 Our fathers trusted in thee: they trusted, and thou didst deliver them. Matt 27:46

5 They cried unto thee, and were delivered: they trusted in thee, and were not confounded.

6 But I *am* a worm, and no man; a reproach of men, and despised of the people. Job 25:6

7 All they that see me laugh me to scorn: they shoot out the lip, they shake the head, *saying*,

8 He trusted on the LORD *that* he would deliver him: let him deliver him, seeing he delighted in him.

9 But thou *art* he that took me out of the womb: thou didst make me hope *when I was* upon my mother's breasts. Ps 71:5-6

10 I was cast upon thee from the womb: thou *art* my God from my mother's belly. Is 49:1

11 Be not far from me; for trouble *is* near; for *there is* none to help.

12 Many bulls have compassed me: strong *bulls* of Bā-shăn have beset me round. Amos 4:1

13 They gaped upon me *with* their mouths, *as* a ravening and a roaring lion.

14 I am poured out like water, and all my bones are out of joint: my heart is like wax; it is melted in the midst of my bowels.

15 My strength is dried up like a potsherd; and my tongue cleaveth to my jaws; and thou hast brought me into the dust of death.

16 For dogs have compassed me: the assembly of the wicked have inclosed me: they pierced my hands and my feet. John 19:34

17 I may tell all my bones: they look *and* stare upon me.

18 They part my garments among them, and cast lots upon my vesture. Matt 27:35

19 But be not thou far from me, O LORD: O my strength, haste thee to help me. Ps 70:5

20 Deliver my soul from the sword; my darling from the power of the dog. Ps 35:17

The Modern Bible, 1990

Although the printing industry has undergone several technological revolutions since Gutenberg, and although color printing is now affordable and ubiquitous, we still read in an antiquated format. A survey of several hundred teenagers by Nelson Publishing found that most don't read the Bible because it's "freaky looking." Most of our Bibles still look like the Geneva Bible, printed in 1590. Shown above is Psalm 22.

have all the technologies we need to create a Renaissance in Bible design - and then not to avail ourselves of them - would be the greatest tragedy of all. We dare not neglect the gifts that are within us!

Many people have sent me emails, saying, "I would love to be able to create my own designer Bible, but I lack the talent." I said the same thing when I began. I studied literature in college and had no prior training in the arts. It still takes me months of painstaking effort to learn a new design program. And then I keep forgetting what I learned and have to start over. But we live in an age whose motto is, "If you can imagine it, you can do it." In fact, the computer removes all barriers and excuses and lays the imagination bare. You can no longer blame your hands or lack of God given talent. The computer gives you a new pair of hands, a technical genius undreamt of by generations past.

"The kingdom of God is within you" (Luke 17:21). We each can build a Kingdom from the gifts inside us. We have only to believe in God, and the strength within us will be released. We can easily forgive previous generations for not designing their books and Bibles in color. It was too difficult and too expensive. But now we possess the keys to the most magnificent kingdom ever granted a generation of writers and designers. We are, quite literally, just a mouse click from our Renaissance.

The truly wise among us have always understood a strange secret about human nature. It is that we too often take our gifts for granted. Just as the writers and illuminators of ages past never dreamed that a man would walk on the moon, they likewise never dreamed of the new technologies that would allow us to create beautiful books and Bibles at such an affordable price. An illuminated Bible from the Middle Ages cost tens of thousands of dollars - or more. We must remind ourselves how special this generation is and how lucky we are to be alive at this very moment. "We must be awake," writes Spurgeon, "for we traverse the enchanted ground." Seldom has a generation traversed such enchanted ground.

Renaissance means rebirth. And so in my lifetime, I will have experienced two rebirths - the one in Christ, the other in the design of our books and Bibles. To the skeptics, I quote **Ephesians 3:20**, in which Paul writes of "**the power that works within us.**" There is no more powerful idea than that of rebirth. This Renaissance is coming, my friends. I may be the least among you, but I have already seen it. I close my eyes and as clearly as when they are open, I see myself in a Christian bookstore in 2015, browsing shelf after shelf of colorfully designed Bibles. I remove one,

Renaissance

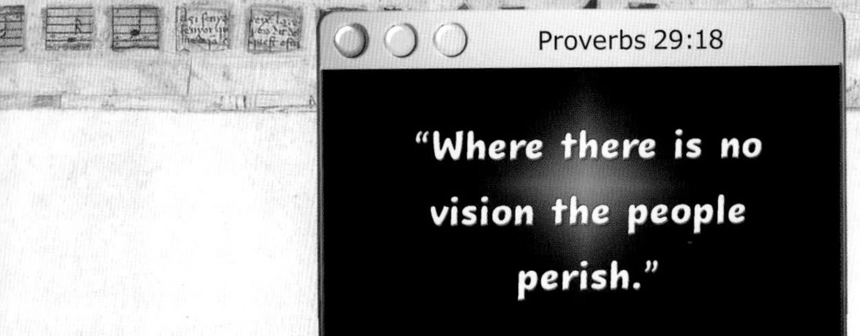
Proverbs 29:18
"Where there is no vision the people perish."

then another, and flip through the pages; they caress my eyes with their resplendent beauty. Genesis, Exodus, Job, Psalms, Proverbs, Gospels, Epistles - I see them all, **thousands of newly designed, colorful Bibles!** I see readers of all ages reclining on sofas, turning the pages of their designer Bibles in a state of rapture, as God's Word touches their souls in glorious new ways! I see children eager to sneak a peak at their parents' Bibles; I even see them quarreling over who gets to read them first!

And I see not just Bibles: I see prayer books, designer devotionals, scholarly treatises, collections of quotations, religious books of all sorts. What a glorious Renaissance awaits us! Shall we journey together? Shall we share in the newness of this visual life? Shall we taste this **heavenly gift?**

Oh, my friends! If you could only see what I see! This Gospel of Matthew is but a baby step, a prelude of the beauty to come!

ruth@dotchrist.net

http://www.christianbookstore.christ
DESIGNER BIBLES™
CLASSICS
252

year: 2015

NEW RELEASES
CLASSICS
.Christ
The Gospel of
Matthew
Beautifully Designed for the Internet Age
OPEN
BEST SELLERS

From Ruth:
Heartfelt thanks to the many wonderful people who generously blessed this project with their time and wisdom. I would like to especially thank the following people for reviewing the artwork, commenting on my testimony, or encouraging me in my faith: John Barnett, David Persson, Steven Szmutko, Lloyd Conway, Ruth Henriquez Lyon, Daniel Maloney, Stephany and Howard Hull, Nancy McClure, Pat and Peter Cook, David and Marti Dunkerton, Merwin Pond, Patricia Mullen, Fran Hamilton, and Zig Ziglar.

This book is dedicated to two of the loveliest people I have met: Gloria and Charlie "Tremendous" Jones. No sooner had I found the Lord than this loving couple blessed my life with such faith and encouragement. They set an example of generosity, passion and commitment to which I can only aspire.

I thank the Lord every day for having blessed me with such loving and devoted business manager, best friend, confidant and husband, Martin, whose encouragement, understanding, and late night conversations (and neck rubs) kept me going no matter my doubts or struggles.

From Alejandra:
"I thank my mother and father, Vivian and Stephen, for giving me life, a life that belongs to my Lord and Savior Jesus Christ."

For more information please visit our website:

www.dotchrist.net

100

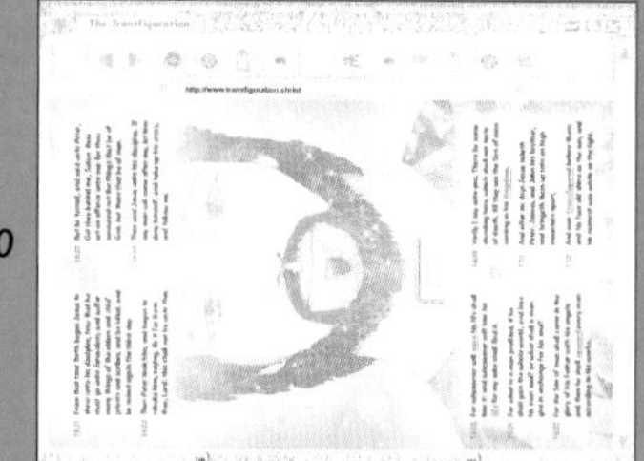

The Transfiguration

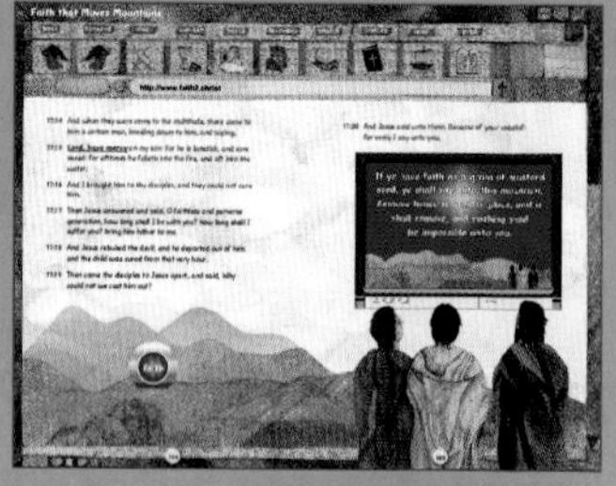

102

Faith that Moves Mountains

110

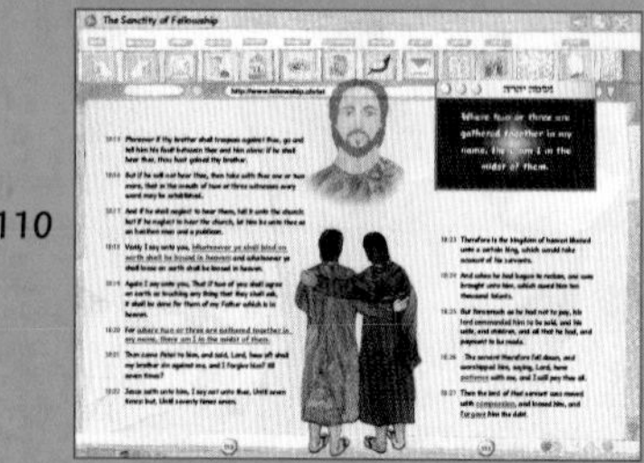

Fellowship in Christ

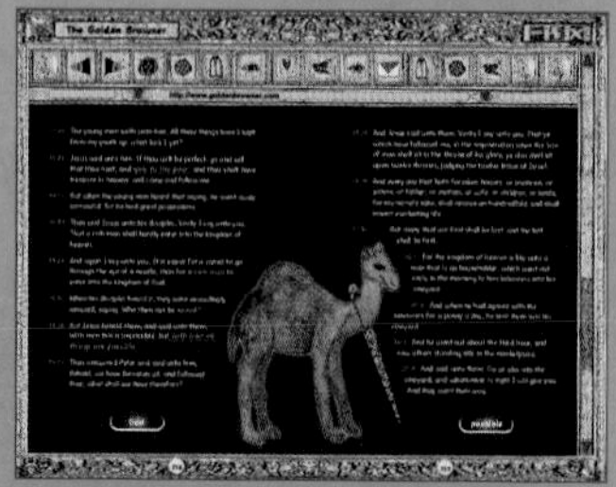

116

The Golden Browser

118

Grace

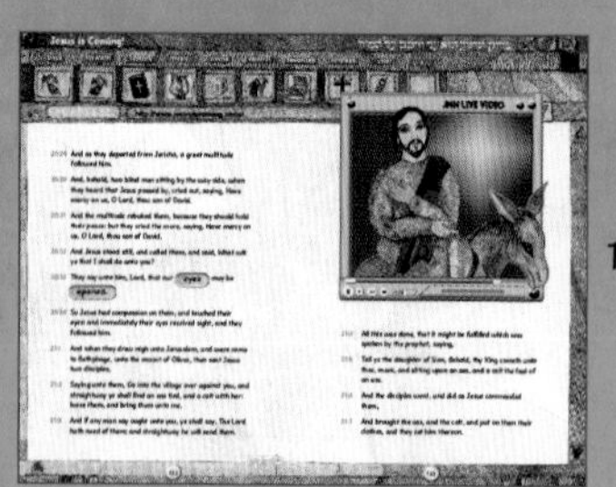

122

Jesus is Coming

128

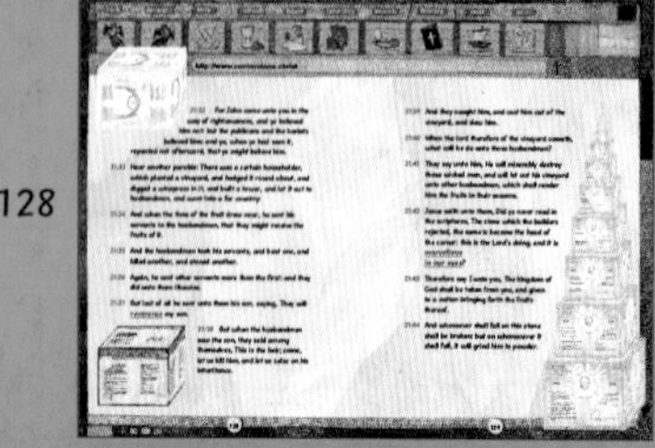

Christ the Cornerstone

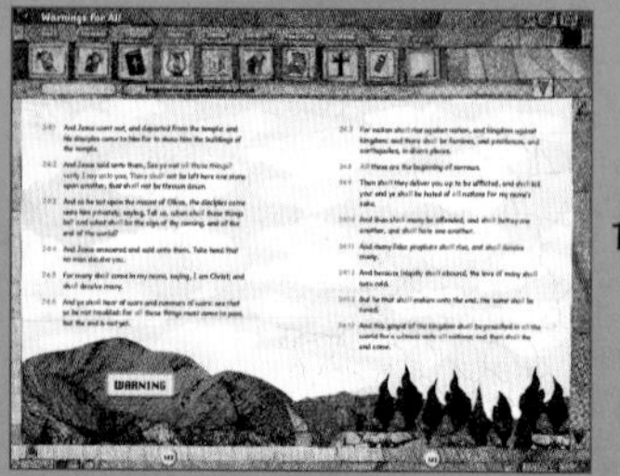

142

Warnings for All